NOBODY HEARD ME CRY

NOBODY HEARD ME CRY

JOHN DEVANE

HACHETTE
BOOKS
IRELAND

First published in Ireland in 2008 by Hachette Books Ireland

1

Copyright © John Devane 2008

The right of John Devane to be identified as the Author of the Work has been asserted by him in accordance with the Copyright, Designs and Patents Act 1988.

A CIP catalogue record for this title is available from the British Library

ISBN 9 780 340 96338 8

Typeset in Sabon MT by Hachette Books Ireland

Printed and bound by Mackays of Chatham Ltd, Chatham, Kent

Hachette Books Ireland policy is to use papers that are natural, renewable and recyclable products and made from wood grown in sustainable forests. The logging and manufacturing processes are expected to conform to the environmental regulations of the country of origin.

Hachette Books Ireland
8 Castlecourt Centre, Castleknock, Dublin 15, Ireland.
A division of Hachette Livre UK Ltd, 338 Euston Road,
London NW1 3BH, England

www.hbgi.ie

CONTENTS

This book is dedicated to my beautiful wife Julieann, who has stuck by me through thick and thin, and who accepted me for the person I am. I also dedicate the book to my two beautiful daughters.

'Let me suffer the pain and shame
I bow my head to their rage and hate,
And I take upon myself the blame.'

Lines from 'Let Me Carry Your Cross for Ireland, Lord!'
by Thomas Ashe

Foreword

This book is an honest attempt to set down the facts of what happened to me in my young life and, in doing so, to try to make some sense of the past that I have run from for many years. In piecing together the painful consequences of an unstable upbringing, my story testifies to just how vulnerable some children are and just how severe the consequences of this can be on young lives.

But the impetus to write the book does not in any way come from a will to reveal unnecessarily the difficult home life that characterised my younger years. Nor do I wish the descriptions of my early years to expose my mother in any way as a bad person. My mother, like many women of her time, struggled and did her best, in her own way, to deal with the enormous challenges that faced her: the upbringing of a large brood of needy children in circumstances of tragedy, followed by poverty. She was operating against the odds, in an often unforgiving and harsh society that made little allowance for the struggles that beset her.

Out of respect to my siblings, I have not included them in any substantial way in this story, recognising their right to privacy. Each child experiences their upbringing in a different way, and I make no claim that my story reflects their own direct experience. Their names, as they appear in this book, are not their real identities.

In portraying the difficulties of my home life as I do in the pages that follow, I merely wish to shed light on the context which, I believe, made me so vulnerable to the sexual abuse that was to follow, outside the home. A small boy, with barely any sense of security or trust in the care of adults – within or outside the home – my fate was sealed: I was easy bait.

I was eight years old when it first began, and this incident marked the beginning of a chain of sexual abuse which, sadly, would continue unabated throughout the remainder of my childhood. I know that my case is not isolated, far from it – although isolated is exactly how I felt at the time these abuses were unfolding. Paedophiles prey on the vulnerability of children, and neglected children are the most vulnerable of all: their voices are the least strong, and the least listened to.

I know that some of this book's contents may be shocking to readers. Indeed, as I set out the facts of my story and relive the horrific events of my hidden past, it still feels shocking even to me. But I truly believe that this story must be told.

I write to lift the lid on the sordid underworld of paedophilia in Ireland, ongoing today. This is just one account in a sea of stories that will never be told. Many victims of abuse never have the opportunity to have their voices heard. Some never cast off their past and carry their vulnerability into adulthood and throughout their whole lives. Others try and fail to take cases against their abusers. It often seems that the law is on the side of the abusers, not the victims.

In 2000, I made a statement to police outlining my years of abuse at the hand of one particular man. I was by now an alcoholic, stumbling from one personal crisis to another. My past was weighing heavily upon me, and I no longer had any choice but to try and deal with it. Attempting to bring my abuser to justice seemed like my only option if I was ever to try and untangle myself from the bitter history of abuse, the consequences of which marred my daily life.

The day I made that statement to gardaí was one of the toughest days of my life. Relating the intimate details of the abuse was traumatic, and I broke down several times, unable to continue. But, each time, I picked myself up and carried on. I was resolved to do this. And, as the words tumbled out over the course of hours, trauma began to give way to relief. It was no longer my sordid secret. I had been brave enough to speak aloud about what had dogged me with shame for too many years to count. I felt validated; I was on my way.

It would be a long wait before the news came that the Director of Public Prosecutions office would not be prosecuting my abuser. As is customary, I would not be privy to the reasons why. On hearing the news, I was plunged into an ever deeper pit of depression. I wanted my abuser to have to pay for what he did to me, and now it seemed that, not for the first time, the law had offered me no sanctuary. I felt as if all avenues had been closed to me, and the anger that raged threatened to drive me over the edge. I wanted to take the law into my own hands, to make him pay, this time on my terms. Thankfully, with the help of friends, I saw the light. Violence would solve nothing.

Instead, I resolved to write this book. I write it for everyone who has felt powerlessness, who has felt silenced. For many years, that was how I felt. I carried around secrets, unable to speak for fear of my life. And I believed, somehow, that I was to blame for what happened to me. But no longer. The time has come to stand up and be counted.

I am one of the lucky ones: I survived. Others are not so fortunate. In 2002, Peter McCloskey revealed the abuse he had suffered at the hands of paedophile priest Father Denis Daly to his family, then to church authorities in Limerick. He wanted to know whether the diocese had reason to suspect that Father Daly, who had died in 1987, might have been a danger to children.

On the eve of this book going to press, the news was broadcast that Pope Benedict XVI was to issue an apology to the victims of clerical abuse in Australia, during his visit there. Father Denis Daly was one of the abusers, moved from Australia to America, then England. Knowledge of his prior investigation by New South Wales police, and subsequent move to Western Australia to avoid prosecution, was not disclosed by the Sydney Diocese, unless fuller details were sought by the new diocese. Thus, he was allowed to be shifted out of sight, to offend elsewhere. Daly was later moved back to Ireland.

Father Daly was the first priest to abuse me, in the public toilets of Limerick's docklands, when I was a young and vulnerable teen. Peter had been raped by the priest during 1980-81, when he was a ten-year-old altar boy.

Over twenty years' on, Peter's search for the truth was met with closed doors, in a defensive and legalistic response from the Limerick Diocese. Peter became increasingly demoralised by the evasiveness of the church authorities. In a letter to one of the churchmen handling his case, he described a recent trip he had made alone to the Sydney archdiocese, to uncover Daly's file, as a 'journey into the valley of Satan himself'.

In 2006, a joint statement was issued by the diocese and Peter's parents, admitting failure on the part of the diocese to properly inform itself of Father Daly's suitability for ministry. But it was too late for Peter. Two days after an earlier, failed mediation meeting with the diocese's representatives, he had taken his own life.

John Devane

In the words of Peter's mother, Mary McCloskey, 'It was the unbearable weight of the denial of the truth that became too much for Peter; that denial must end.'

I write this for him.

John Devane
July 2008

Prologue

It's a chilly, drizzly night, way past midnight, when I finally reach the bleak Limerick police station. My heart pounds and my mouth is dry as I approach the reception desk. It's piled high with paperwork, and the garda, whom I know, rouses himself to greet me.

'Where is he?' I ask urgently.

The guard hands over a newly handwritten charge sheet. 'Usual barmy Saturday night.' He smiles wryly and stretches.

We exchange comradely nods but, tonight, I'm not interested in small talk and hardly hear him. My hand shakes a little but my face remains expressionless when I accept the sheet and glance over the contents. I focus on the name and draw a deep breath. I've waited so long for this opportunity, and now that it has arrived I feel as though I've won the Lotto.

A manilla folder reveals a photo of a youth with short dark hair. He's beaming innocently at the camera and carries a puppy in his arms. He looks about fourteen years of age.

'Says he wasn't aware,' the guard remarks sarcastically. He's seen it all before.

I nod in agreement. I'm itching to move on. As he retrieves his keys from his pocket, I'm already striding down the bright, dingy yellow corridor. When I peer through the smeared window of the interview room, I see a seemingly harmless middle-aged man with a reddish goatee beard. He's sitting at a screwed-down metal table, his face in his hands, elbows on the surface. Tufts of gingery hair poke out from behind his ears and the fluorescent light flickers above him, reflecting eerily off his balding head.

I clench my jaw but maintain my composure as the guard turns the key. The man looks up. The scent of stale sweat and fear instantly hits my nostrils. His eyes are the same watery blue that I remember. He had a full head of red hair back then but his usual flamboyant taste in clothes hasn't changed. He's dressed in a satiny cornflower-blue suit and an elaborate glittery waistcoat.

Our gaze meets across the table as the door closes behind me with a deadening clunk. He straightens in his chair and makes a weak attempt to smile. I move towards the table and sit opposite him. In my dark pinstripe suit and crisp white shirt I look exactly like a lawyer about to interview his client. Yet, beneath my professional veneer, my heart beats so hard I'm sure he can hear it.

I know his name. We've met in amateur dramatics' circles over the years and, with this link, he's confident I'm there to help him. But, unknown to him, we also met when I was a young boy. I know his past but he, as yet, is unaware of mine.

He leans forward and interlocks his fingers, his knuckles white. His lower jaw trembles before he speaks. 'They've got me here under false pretences, John. He swore he was eighteen, so help me God.' He moistens his lips with his tongue and runs his hand through his thinning hair.

I hold on to my anger, allow it to seethe but not to escape. I need to remain in control of this situation. 'So, you're saying you didn't know he was fifteen?'

He loosens his tie with one hand. His tone is imploring. 'Jesus, John, I swear to God, if you saw photographs of this person – I could show them to you, I've photographs of him up at the house . . .'

I'm sure you have, I think, as I take out the picture of the youth from the folder and push it across the table towards him. 'You really thought he was eighteen?' I say.

'John, I swear on my mother's life . . . it's all a terrible mistake.' He avoids looking down at the photo.

'Is that him?' I watch his reaction as his eyes flick down, then quickly away. He nods briefly and leans over the table, still protesting his innocence.

'So, has this ever happened to you with an underage young person before?' I enquire.

He looks outraged. 'No, no, no, no, John. Jesus, no. I'm gay, but I don't go for kids. No, I'd never go for kids.'

I have to give it to him, it's a fine performance. It might even convince a judge, or a jury. But it cuts no ice with me.

My stomach churns. It's almost impossible to remain calm. I stare at my fingernails. They could do with a trim. I like to keep them clean and short, well manicured. I feign indifference as I glance up and meet his gaze.

Despite his assurances, he's sweating. I'm sweating also, but it's a cold sweat. 'Are you absolutely sure? Because . . . you know . . . a lot could depend on it.'

He is shaking with fear, and his eyes fill with tears. 'I swear to you, John, I had absolutely no idea . . .'

'I'll have to stop you there. Because, unfortunately, that's not how I see it . . .'

He wipes his eyes, all ears. 'What? Surely it depends on how we defend this thing?'

'This thing.' Is that how he sees it? I shuffle my papers and look through the notes. The overhead light flickers as he, unable to stop fidgeting, undoes the top button of his shirt. I relish his discomfort as I continue to interrogate him. 'You say you'd no idea he was underage. And that you don't make a habit of picking up young men?'

'John . . . I swear to God . . . you've known me for years now . . .'

'That's true. And that's why I believe you're lying to me.' I'm tired of his game, anxious to cut to the chase. I take a deep breath. At last I'm able to release the words that have been locked inside me for so long. 'Let me take you back about thirty years,' I speak quietly. 'It was a drizzly night, rather like this one. At eleven , you picked up a young boy in Castletroy. He was only a young teenager . . . yet you offered him a place in your perverted bed.'

He looks like he's been shot, his mouth open, his eyes widening in memory. 'Oh, fuck' is written across his forehead, as clear as if it were pulsing in neon.

'The chemist's son?' he blurts out.

'Indeed, that's what you thought,' I reply. ' "Aren't you the chemist's son," you asked after you picked me up. But I wasn't the chemist's son, was I? I was a frightened kid in trouble. I told you I was running away to Dublin . . . remember?'

He's dumbstruck, hanging on to my every word. I have him right in the palm of my hand. I want to run around the room, whooping and shouting like a footballer who's scored the winning goal. Instead, I stick to my plan. I need to play a long game here, just like he has done himself, throughout the years. He's sitting back, blasted with shock, his breathing shallow. 'Oh my God. Oh shit, oh fuck,' he begins, but I interrupt him again.

'I also remember how you used to call boys like me "chicken". It amused you. You said you could get "plenty of chicken", as much as you could eat, whenever you wanted. You said you especially liked Turkish chicken or Russian chicken . . . remember?.' His face is ashen but he's listening intently. 'I remember everything about you, especially how you lay on top of me and forced me to do exactly what you did to this young boy whose life you've ruined.'

'Oh my God . . .' He can't stop blabbering. 'I never meant . . . all those times we met . . . why didn't you say something?'

'Who would have believed me?' I ask. 'And, anyway, I knew my time would come . . . eventually. You know what they say about a dish best served cold? Well, this "chicken" is now serving you back.'

This is what I've always wanted, to see him thunderstruck and terrified, no longer the confident, strutting personality with an unblemished record. I make no attempt to break the silence that follows. After a long pause, he clears his throat. 'So . . . er . . . oh God . . . does this change things between us John? Are you still, well, able to be my solicitor?'

I should have been surprised by his question but I always knew his main concern would be to save his own skin.

'Well, that depends,' I reply. 'But I can't be your solicitor if you carry on lying to the guards and denying that you abused this young man – because he is another "chicken", like I was, isn't he?'

He squirms in his chair, searching for words. I stand up and swipe the file off the table. He's not the only one who can act. 'So, you have a choice. You carry on lying, and I'll walk out that door and tell the guards I can't take on your case because there is a conflict of interest. Whatever has been said in here stays in here. I will then take some time to consider my own next move, given our *history*. Or, you can make a statement to the gardaí telling the truth.'

He rubs both hands over his sweating scalp. 'I don't have a choice, do I?'

'On the contrary, the choice is all yours,' I tell him.

'And you'll definitely still represent me?' he asks.

'Make your statement, Seamus, and we'll see.'

He's desperate, dreading what his future holds. That future is in his own hands, and he now knows about our past. Yet he still wants me to represent him. I don't try to fathom his reasons. It's difficult enough to fathom my own but I know what I must do. I'm a defence lawyer, a good one. I suddenly see myself as if from above: a professional man, in control, imposing and cool. So much for outward appearances.

When I was young boy, I saw Gregory Peck in *To Kill a Mockingbird*. I never forgot that film, the study of a strong, righteous man seeking the truth. Gregory Peck is a distant relative of my father, or so I've been told, and, perhaps, he's the reason I decided to become a lawyer. But he was only acting the part, just as I'm acting now by allowing this pathetic, whining man to stew in his own misery. I know his past, unlike the next potential defence lawyer he'll hire if I refuse to represent him. He can't lie and hide the truth from me. I'm his truth, just as countless other young men were victims of his deceit, hypocrisy and perversion. Yes, I'll agree to defend him, but it will be on the terms I've outlined. I'll do my job and let justice decide what becomes of him.

Why don't I come clean, destroy him utterly by revealing my own story? It's a rhetorical question. I know the answer. I've clawed my way out of a sordid, abusive past and confronted my demons on the way. But I'm still not ready for a public confession, the sensation that will follow such a revelation. Like all victims, guilt clings to me like a second skin, the feeling it could all have been avoided if only I had been born a different person. A good person. Someone who did not attract the men who used my body and tried to destroy my mind. I've built a successful career, acquired the trappings to go with this lifestyle.

But, inwardly, I'm still that lost child, unable to step outside the degrading memories. Some day I'll be strong enough to do what is necessary but tonight has given me a small victory. I've taken a step forward and haven't faltered. I open the door of Seamus Connery's cell. He's still watching me. His eyes bore into my back. But, as I snap the door behind me, I can't ever remember any other occasion when I held my head as high.

1

Runway to Love

As a city, Limerick has a tough reputation. Sitting on the Shannon estuary, in the south-west of Ireland, it was well established as a rugged manufacturing town with thriving docks when my parents first met in the 1940s. At that time, the population was around 60,000 and Limerick was a city of life, music and poetry, full of hard workers and hard graft.

It was also a city of ships. They carried cattle, tobacco, sugar and other goods that supplied Clunes Tobacco works, the tanneries and abattoirs, and the famous Limerick ham. The factory that made Cleve's toffee, beloved by generations of children, was a landmark, with its huge factory chimney, now demolished. The sweet factory was only one of a range of manufacturing companies that attracted people from the surrounding countryside and coastal areas to the city in search of work.

My parents met shortly after the Second World War when jobs were scarce and the Depression sat heavily on the population. My mother, Agnes Wallace, was a town girl, born and bred. Wallace is a name synonymous with shoemaking over generations, and Agnes came from a long line of shoemakers who were famous in Limerick City.

My mother was the baby of the family. She had six big brothers and an older sister, Nora, who ended up running a guesthouse. One brother escaped to England and never came back, but the rest remained at home. They were reared under an extremely tough regime. My grandmother was very hard on her children and had a reputation as a strict disciplinarian, who 'ruled by the leather strap'. My grandfather ran his successful shoemaking business, training two of his sons to take over. All the men drank heavily, as was the custom at the time. It was a case of work hard, play hard and repent on a Sunday.

Agnes was sent out to earn her living at the age of fourteen. Further education was not an option, and this was typical treatment for working-class girls in the early 1940s. Shannon Airport was just being commercialised, and she got a job waiting tables in the restaurant. This was where, five years' later, she met my father, Michael Devane, who came from a very different background.

His family hailed from what is, to my mind, the most beautiful place in Ireland. Situated on the far south-west tip of the country, Dingle is a picturesque fishing village. His family had been in the fishing trade for generations; his three brothers, his father and grandfather were Dingle fishermen who owned their own boats. His mother, Mary Ashe, also known as Minnie Ashe, was the sister of Thomas Ashe, the famous Irish patriot.

Thomas was a teacher, who took part in the Easter Rising in Dublin in 1916. Despite being captured and imprisoned, court-martialled and, finally, released under a General Amnesty in 1917, he remained politically active. He was accused of sedition after giving a speech at Ballinalee and was convicted on the evidence of police 'mental note takers'. Sentenced to two years' in Mountjoy Gaol, he went on hunger strike as a protest against the criminal status of republican prisoners. For refusing food, his bed, bedding and boots were removed by the prison authorities. After six days, while still refusing to eat, he was forcibly fed. Weakened and unable to endure this procedure, he was blue in the face and unconscious when he was returned to his cell. He later died, six hours after being admitted to hospital.

His inquest lasted eleven days and was one of the most sensational in history. According to medical evidence, he died of heart failure and congestion of the lungs, brought on by the removal of his bed and being forced to lie on the cold floor for fifty hours before being subjected to forcible feeding. The inquest condemned forcible or mechanical feedings as an inhuman and dangerous operation that should be discontinued. The authorities were accused of not acting more promptly and of using an assistant doctor who had no previous practice in administering forcible feeding.

My father's family had valid reasons for being proud of their patriotic relation. By his actions and untimely death, Thomas Ashe won the prisoners' fight for political status. His funeral attracted over forty thousand people who walked the streets of Dublin in his honour. Michael Collins, the renowned republican who would also die later in tragic circumstances, delivered his funeral oration.

As a result of this historical legacy, my father, despite being a simple working man, was well read and quite politicised. During the war, he joined the army. His superior officer, recognising his intelligence and his connections to Thomas Ashe, offered him training as an aircraft mechanic. He was sent to train at Naas, a town just outside Dublin, which was how he later ended up at Shannon Airport five years later where my mother was still working.

My mother was nineteen when that first meeting took place. My father was twenty-eight but, despite a nine-year gap, their attraction was instant and powerful. Agnes was petite and attractive, with dark hair, blue eyes and a striking figure. She was chatty and affable when she served him in the restaurant. He was up from the country, she was a town girl and, as opposites attract, they hit it off immediately.

Later, they met again in the Stella Ballroom in Limerick where most of the eligible young people gathered on a typical Saturday night. I imagine her in a neat, knee-length crepe dress, her long dark hair curled for the occasion; and he in a stiff collar and tie, his dark hair slicked back, his face freshly shaven, his blue eyes lighting up when he recognised her from the opposite side of the hall. He would have been amusing and flirtatious as they danced together, perhaps both of them realising that this was the start of their lives together.

When Agnes got home that night, she couldn't stop talking about the handsome young man whose uncle was the patriot Thomas Ashe. To the Wallace family, Thomas Ashe was a hero who had stood up to the English oppressors and died for his country. When Agnes invited Michael home to meet her mother, Grandmother Wallace was a delightful hostess, eager to impress. However, my mother was embarrassed and ashamed that her new boyfriend was taking tea in her end-of-terrace house, in a parlour which doubled up as a shoe workshop. She wanted to have a better life, and this mature, attractive man could be the way to achieve it. She was also a fairly strong-willed personality, even at that young age.

Although my mother's family was established as hard-working tradespeople, the Thomas Ashe connection, and his white-collar job put my father above them socially. These snobbish distinctions were part of life in those difficult times. To her family, her marriage was a step up, but to my father's family, it was a step down. Despite any perceived class or age difference, my parents fell passionately in love and, within a year, were married in a simple ceremony at the Dominican Church in Limerick.

At the time of her marriage, Agnes was doing well in her job at the airport, and the restaurant manager pleaded with her to stay. He believed she had managerial potential and offered to train her further, even to put her through night school. However, as was common practice at the time, she had to leave work once she married in 1947. Although my mother has never disclosed much about her history, she says she never regretted getting married, especially to Michael Devane. But she did regret being denied the career opportunities that were open to her. Once wed, she had to knuckle down to married life, whether she liked it or not.

Even after their simple marriage ceremony, my parents continued their passionate affair. They were lovers, first and foremost and, according to my older sisters, they would often disappear into their bedroom in the little rented flat in Mallow Street and, later, Thomas Street. Not surprisingly, within a year of marriage, a first baby was born, my eldest brother Declan. He was a beautiful boy with golden curls and an angelic face. After his birth, they moved to their first rented house, called Iona, on the Carey's Road in central Limerick. My father continued working at the airport as an aircraft mechanic for the next thirteen years.

Apart from a six-year gap between numbers five and six, my mother had a child almost every year between Declan's birth in 1949 and mine in 1962. Declan was followed by four girls: Angela, Sorcha, Deirdre and Grainne. Then, after the six-year gap, she had two belated children. Bernard was born first and, eighteen months later, myself, the last child to land into this large, unruly Catholic family. My parents named me John after one of my uncles, who later died when I was three.

I'd like to say that I was a deeply loved and wanted child and that my early life was happy and carefree. Unfortunately, due to circumstances over which no one, expect Fate, had any control, this was not the case. It sounds harsh when I write it down, and I don't believe for a moment that Agnes set out to deliberately make my life unhappy. That would be absurd. Life is much more random and complex than that and, given the tragic events that were to blight my family's early years, I think she was largely helpless in the face of dire, unforeseen consequences.

In an effort to understand the tragic environment that changed my formative years, and marked the lives of my siblings, I need to go back to an earlier time, an event that I believe profoundly affected my mother. When she was twelve years old, her own father collapsed dramatically during a rugby match at the Shannon Rugby Club. My grandfather, who was only fifty-six when he died, used to work on the sidelines as part of the match crew. He was taken ill, literally on the sidelines, and was pronounced dead by the time he reached the hospital.

Agnes, the youngest in the family, was devastated. She had been the apple of her daddy's eye, his special pet, and he had doted on her. His early and unforeseen death put a great deal of strain on his family. Two of Agnes's brothers, whom she idolised, were forced to take over the family business just as the Second World War began in 1939. The shock of my grandmother's bereavement made her harsher still. She ruled the roost with a tight hard fist, beating her children into obedience and pushing her two sons into working long hours in the family business. Perhaps it's not insignificant that two of her sons suffered nervous breakdowns. One was institutionalised for the rest of his life. The other brothers escaped into drink, one of them finding relief through Alcoholics Anonymous. Through the untimely death of my grandfather, what had been a harsh but, for those times, a relatively ordinary family life, became dysfunctional in a way that would have lasting effects on my mother.

My father had a gentle personality. To the best of my knowledge, he never hit his children and was a ray of light around the house. Often my mother and he would stay up all night, chatting and flirting, and she often slept late in the morning as a result. He got into the habit of bringing her up a cup of tea and a slice of toast every morning before he set out for Shannon. She was waited on hand and foot.

He didn't drink, but over the years he became a secret gambler. He also smoked like a trooper, which didn't do his health any good. He began to work nights on a regular basis, earning extra income which, perhaps, gave him more freedom to do whatever he liked away from home. He started attending the races regularly. Agnes was still in love with him and didn't question his judgement or actions.

She never knew how much he earned, although he always gave her more than enough to pay the bills and clothe and feed us. The fridge was full, and we had clean clothes. Every morning, he would coax his children from bed and get them organised. But then he disappeared for the rest of the day. My mother had achieved what she desired. She had moved a step up in life by marrying him, and I suppose she accepted her lot – or did her best to manage, even when she had reason to feel insecure.

During the early years of their marriage, my father accepted a contract to work in Iceland for six months as a mechanic for Pan Am. The money was good and it gave him an opportunity to escape from the incessant demands of Limerick family life. Whatever his reasons, I've been told that one night when my mother phoned his hotel room, the phone was answered by a woman.

Agnes was utterly shocked and upset but, on his return, my father was able to smooth it all over with his disarming charm, saying, 'We were all in my room that night, having a bit of a party.' He told her that she was 'just one of the girls on his team'. He also made sure his colleagues backed him up when my mother questioned them. She eventually swallowed this story. She wanted to trust him implicitly but, in retrospect, I think he was more than a bit economical with the truth. He told my mother one thing and did another, especially when it came to the horses. One of my sisters recalls how he brought her a stick of rock from the races, saying 'Don't tell Mammy.' I imagine, 'Don't tell Mammy' was a phrase repeated more often than Agnes realised.

His charm, and ability to sing, entertain and make love passionately, probably papered over the cracks in their marriage, especially when my mother's temper was frayed from having to take care of six children under twelve. My parents were still relatively happy and prospering when they moved in 1960 to a new housing estate in Ballykeefe, north of Limerick City. My father now had a bigger house on a mortgage and life was hectic. Agnes was a good cook and the family enjoyed regular mealtimes round the table.

I was born in 1962 when Agnes was thirty-five. From all accounts, she had a relatively easy pregnancy. Despite being an 'accident', I sense that I was happy swimming around inside her womb before being launched into the world in St Munchin's Hospital on a chilly autumn day. My parents had resigned themselves to having another mouth to feed, but it must have been difficult, especially as it was only eighteen months since their last child, Bernard, was born. However, my sisters tell me I was a beautiful baby who seldom cried. My father enjoyed picking me up, feeding me the odd bottle, and singing to me softly in his Gaelic tenor voice.

Everything seemed to go well enough at first. But history was about to repeat itself in the most dreadful manner imaginable for my mother. Indeed, without warning, all our lives would be smashed into smithereens, and nothing in the Devane family would ever be the same again.

2

Tragedy Strikes

I was only six weeks old when tragedy struck, so I must depend on the recollections of my siblings, particularly my middle sister Deirdre, to chart this train of events.

The twenty-fourth of November of that year was a typically icy, wintry day with grey clouds hanging heavily over the distant hills of County Clare. As usual, most of my six siblings were at school. Bernard was toddling around the kitchen and I was tucked up snugly in the family's battered old Moses basket.

My father was home that morning, dozing. Around lunchtime, he complained of chest pains. When the pain did not subside, my mother called the ambulance, and he was rushed away to St John's Hospital. My sisters remember to this day seeing the ambulance pass them as they were on their way home from school. They had no idea it was carrying their father.

My mother stayed in the hospital through that afternoon and into the long evening. She came home long after teatime and put us to bed. Then, at around eleven o'clock, the telephone rang. Hands trembling, my mother picked up the receiver.

It was the hospital. My father had suffered a second heart attack, and this one was fatal. At forty-four years of age, he was dead. A doctor explained that the heavy smoking had weakened his heart to such an extent that there was nothing they could do to help. The second attack had been a massive one.

Mammy fell apart completely. 'Oh, dear Lord Jesus, not my darling Michael, please God, no.' She was inconsolable, despite Declan's efforts to comfort her, even as tears ran down his own cheeks. The following morning, Declan had to shoulder his first new responsibility as head of the house-hold. He had to break the news to my sisters that their father was not coming home.

For my mother, who had lost her own father to a similar fate, it must have seemed unbearable for history to repeat itself in this way. She must have asked herself why the men in her life died so young. Why did the very ones who brought her laughter, love and happiness have to be taken away so suddenly, in such an awful way?

Mammy must have wondered if there had been anything she could have done to save her precious husband. She now had so many mouths to feed, all on her own. How would she cope? And she had a sick toddler and a brand-new baby drawing on her, as well.

Bernard had been only six months old when he was diagnosed with cancer. It had been a tough time for my parents and now she would have to handle his illness on her own. Bernard spent the next five years receiving treatment, which was ultimately successful. But she had no way of knowing what the future held for her. As for me, I would never know my father. Six weeks old and snug in my Moses basket, I was unaware that the sun had gone down on the Devane household.

Agnes had no real close family to call on for help. Her relationship with her own mother was a difficult one. Her sister Nora was very busy with her own business and family, and Daddy's wider family was far away in Dingle. Plus, they had never really approved of him marrying beneath him, so my mother couldn't really turn to them for support.

My mother and her children must have sat there, stunned, trying to understand that they would never see Daddy again. Only the previous morning, they'd watched him singing cheerfully to himself when they set out for school. He'd probably been cracking a joke or laughing as he made tea for Mammy and brought it to her bedside, just as he always did. As he would never do again. How indestructible he must have seemed when he kissed her on the lips and thundered downstairs, full of energy.

His sudden death seemed utterly futile. His funeral was a

large one. But my sister Deirdre missed it; she was at home minding Bernard and me.

After his funeral, my older sisters tell me that Agnes took to her bed a great deal, unable to get up and dressed. She seemed incapable of functioning under the weight of grief and, from what I can gather, appeared to slip into a deep depression.

What was once a happy, orderly household soon became chaotic. Mealtimes were forgotten, washing left, chores undone. It must have been a terrifying time as the older children tried to make sense of what had happened and keep things going for the younger ones.

But worse was to come. Agnes had adored her husband, but it wasn't just his presence that was taken from her so suddenly and irrevocably. As she quickly discovered, no provision had been made for his family if he died in an accident or of natural causes. Our security and our livelihood were gone in an instant.

Who expects to die suddenly at forty-four? My father was not a bad man, nor was he thoughtless. I can't get angry with him because I know from those whose lives he touched that he was a likeable, colourful character. He had tried to make up for any shortage of money by always being 'on call' to pick up another job at the airport. Perhaps he was stressed, not getting enough sleep, overworking and worried deep down about money. What's clear is that he was burning the candle at both ends, supporting a house full of kids while maintaining an expensive secret life. I suspect that any excess money he earned went straight on the horses. He certainly didn't invest it into something as boring and sensible as life insurance. He was superstitious and, ironically, he felt that if he took out life insurance, it was a bad omen and would somehow mysteriously hasten his death. So, part of me understands well. But, nonetheless, it must have been deeply humiliating to my mother that she and her family had been so far down on his list of priorities not only in life but also now in death.

Despite her grief, Agnes did try to cope. She got a job working nights in a hospital, but quickly realised she wasn't bringing in enough to cover the mortgage repayments. The consequence of this was that we were forced to move from our house on the Ballykeefe estate back to Marian Avenue, in Janesboro. This was where they lived before my father successfully managed to move us up in the world. Marian Avenue was a street of grey council houses in a rough part of town. All my siblings were still under thirteen, and we were now seriously poor. Agnes had only about eleven shillings a week from her widow's pension to live on, to feed us all and to manage her large household.

The Christmas of 1962 was particularly grim for the Devane family. The usual festive celebrations, where my father would be full of Christmas cheer, were extremely muted, with few decorations, no tree and only sparse presents. At one point in early 1963, I was actually fostered by another family, the Garretts, who took me off Mammy's hands to allow her a few weeks' welcome respite.

But life had to go on. Spring turned into summer and a sort of normality resumed. The older children went to school and tried to do their daily homework. The middle children prepared for their Confirmations and we all attended mass on Sundays. It was a struggle to make ends meet, and the constant need to wash clothes, prepare meals with whatever scant food there was and deal with a small house crammed with growing kids was more than my mother could bear.

She remained depressed. It was a struggle for her to rise in the morning and, understandably, she increasingly depended on both Declan and Deirdre to be the household's mini-father and -mother.

The children, who had been so relatively happy whilst my father had been alive, now squabbled all the time. The peacemaker was gone from our home, and no doubt they were also taking their cue from their mother, who was increasingly intolerant towards them.

If I had a magic wand, I would wish dearly to change the history of those early years of my life. But changing the past is impossible. Trying to understand and learn from the experience is the best we can do. As an adult, I began to try and fathom how this dysfunctional environment played a part in my path of addictive self-destruction and abuse. How could I blame anyone? We were a family in mourning, with few comforts and no one to help us.

Yet, this I do know. Love is the most important thing a child needs to feel emotionally and physically secure. This security creates self-confidence, high self-esteem and well-being. Perhaps, had things been different, if life had gone the way my parents believed it would go, my mother would have found space for me in her heart. As it was, I remained outside her affection while she struggled to find a way out of the grief that overwhelmed her.

My older siblings staggered on, going out to get Saturday jobs and paper rounds, scrounging and drudging to make ends meet. But at least we had each other. By September 1963, I was sitting up, crawling and generally 'into everything', a typical eleven-month-old baby. I was keen to walk early and cruised around the furniture, shuffling along on my tiny feet, straining for independence. I was mostly carried around by Deirdre and felt that I bonded with her as if she was my real mother. My other sisters also changed my nappies and gave me bottles of water to suck on, for milk and solid food were not always freely available.

Things might eventually have improved, in time, when the shock waves abated. But, sadly, that was not to be. What followed hot on the heels of Daddy's death could not have been foreseen by anyone and would seal our fate as a family marked by misfortune.

3

Fallen Angel

My brother Declan was thirteen when my father died. Bookish and spiritual, he was an altar boy with a sweet singing voice. Although he'd been born with a club foot, which had never been corrected, he overcame this disability with typical fortitude. He joined in sporting activities and cycled to and from school, just like any other kid on our street. Most importantly, he could soothe my mother in her almost inconsolable grief. Declan did many of the household chores, pushing laundry into the twin tub in the kitchen with the tongs or hanging it out in the garden. He would sweep and clean, just like the girls. He took on the role as head of the household, a replacement father to us all, and he took his duties very seriously indeed.

Agnes worked long nights at the hospital. As a result, she generally slept mornings. The older children tiptoed around, getting up and ready for school, or tending to me and Bernard. Deirdre was often left in charge of us overnight, a hefty responsibility for a nine year old, while Declan ran the household on a practical level, rather like a caretaker.

The afternoon of 17 September 1963 was crisp and autumnal. My three sisters were at school; they had sandwiches, but Declan, who went to a different school, always cycled home for lunch. This time, he was late.

Some time had passed after he was due home when a car pulled up outside our gate. This was unusual, as cars were not as plentiful back then. Mammy, by now no doubt concerned as to Declan's whereabouts, was drawn instantly to the door upon hearing the car. The door of the car opened, and two priests stepped out, along with the school nurse. My mother's face creased with worry. The two priests took her into the parlour, while the school nurse pottered around the kitchen, washing the dishes. She was at that when my sisters came home from school. They could hear the unnatural silence in the house, punctuated by wails from my mother.

The news was bad. Declan had left the school at lunchtime, on his bicycle. Then there had been an accident. Mother disappeared with the priests, whisked to his side at the hospital.

Several hours later, we were huddled together in the front parlour, a cheerless, chilly, wallpapered room that we rarely went into. It was dark by now, and Deirdre was on the lookout for Mammy to come home.

When finally Mammy did arrive back, the terrible news was broken. Declan was dead. Our beloved, beautiful Declan, the busy young boy, full of life, always busy, had died in a terrible road accident.

He'd come rushing out of school, like any normal schoolboy of fourteen, satchel slung over his back. He'd jumped on his black Raleigh bicycle, turned right out of school and cycled directly into the path of an oncoming saloon car. He was hit full on, with an impact that knocked him so hard that he was flung over the bonnet of the car, smashed into the windscreen and then landed in a crumpled heap beside the driver's door. The driver screeched to an abrupt halt, but it was too late.

Shocked bystanders rushed to Declan's side to administer first aid, but he had sustained horrendous multiple internal injuries. He was rushed to the Regional Hospital in Dooradoyle, and doctors had worked on his broken body for four hours. But it was hopeless. He lost the struggle for life. His angelic face was barely scratched, his golden curls hardly tousled, but his internal injuries were so severe that his heart had given up. The nurses said he looked like a fallen angel.

Sadly, my mother was too distraught to say a final good-bye from the mortuary to her beautiful first son. My aunt Nora and Nana went to the removal, along with my older sisters. That image of a mother, unable to face her dead son on the start of his final journey, always evokes a great sense of sadness in me. The other notable absentee was Deirdre; once again, she was at home minding Bernard and me.

But my mother did attend the funeral, which was huge. The death of any young person touches the entire community. All his school and people from every club where he was a member came to pay their respects. Everyone who was at my father's funeral was there.

The winter of 1963 was utterly bleak. Our family was buried under a layer of despair as deep as arctic snow. In less than a year, my father had dropped dead, my eldest brother had been run over and killed. The assassination of President Kennedy threw the world into chaos, and our small world – at Marian Avenue – was no less chaotic. We had become a downward-spiralling, fragmented family, weighed down by bitterness, gloom and grief. On top of the two untimely deaths of our loved ones, my mother was struggling to cope with Bernard's cancer. At that time, having cancer was a frightening prospect and, unlike today, treatments were more basic and the survival rate was low.

My mother was so punch-drunk from the pain of loss that she must have functioned as an automaton as she took Bernard to St Munchin's Hospital, where she still worked nights, for long sessions of radiotherapy. I've no doubt she was convinced he would go the way of her husband and eldest son. Why should she think otherwise? She had faced her worst possible nightmares and had seen them come true. She had nothing left inside her to give, especially to me, her youngest child. Increasingly, Mammy became angry and resentful.

As she coped with Bernard and his treatments, more chores fell on the shoulders of my sisters. They were so young for this responsibility and squabbled incessantly with each other. Increasingly, Deirdre shouldered more and more responsibility. She moaned the least while doing the most. I was at the bottom of the pecking order and was left alone a lot of the time, receiving little attention from my preoccupied mother and overstrained sisters. We had to tiptoe round Bernard, who had extra-special treatment: the best place on the sofa, the nicest food, the warmest water to wash in. Even though he was sick, his special treatment did cause resentments among my siblings.

We were also quite cramped for space in our council house, which didn't improve family relations, especially with a household of growing girls who needed space. Angela and Sorcha shared the upstairs front bedroom, while Deirdre and Grainne had the little back boxroom. My brother slept on a camp bed in my mother's room, and I shared her bed with her.

It was a very basic bedroom, with a wooden kitchen chair, which doubled as a bedside table, on Mammy's side of the bed, and only a thin blanket and sheet. There was a flimsy brown veneer wardrobe, with my mother's few clothes in it, and a little dressing table, but she didn't have anything in the way of cosmetics or perfume.

It might seem that sleeping with my mother put me in a priv-
ileged position – and, to some extent, it did. But Mammy was
never affectionate towards me. In fact, the opposite, if anything,
was the reality. That was just the way it was. And, although I
knew better than to disturb her, I still longed for her touch.

But, despite this, when I was in bed with her, I felt safe.
It's probably the only memory I have of feeling that way
when I was a child.

Just as Daddy had brought my mother her morning cup
of tea, we children now took on this task. Mammy would be
in a deep sleep after her night shift, and the children would
tiptoe around getting ready for school. Finally, the daily cup
of tea would be brought to her bedside in order to rouse her.

She was very particular about her tea. She liked to drink
it from a white mug, with two spoons of sugar, along with
two slices of toast, with Kerrygold butter and jam on the
side. I was five when I first began to do the tea routine. I
would walk up the stairs holding on to the mug by its handle,
with the saucer balanced on top. That was to keep the tea
warm. I'd put her tea and toast on the chair beside her bed,
and she'd rouse herself. I'd move away to the door and watch
gingerly as she took her first sip. Was it OK? Was it hot
enough? Had I done it right? If she wasn't pleased, there
could be hell to pay.

The fear I was beginning to feel towards Mammy was
exacerbated when an incident happened involving our cat
Tibs. I remember him jumping up on the bed to us one night

– strictly not allowed. My mother grabbed him by the back of the neck and threw him roughly out the door. I was very small, probably no more than two or three, and as I watched the animal scamper off, frightened, I worried that if I did something my mother didn't like, she would grab me by the back of the neck and throw me out of the door, just like Tibs. I felt that, to her, I was just another needy, annoying animal who needed controlling.

Even so, I saw a kinder side to Mammy as she tended to my brother during his illness. She would put a cushion behind his head on the sofa or give him a cuddle or stroke his hair. He lapped up this extra cosseting. And, although I knew this special treatment was justified, it felt unfair. I felt that, to Mammy, I was invisible, or a nuisance.

Bedtime was seven o'clock, regardless of the season or the occasion. I would be put to bed every night in Mammy's bedroom by one of my sisters, who took it in turns. The procedure was always the same. Bernard and myself would be tucked in, our sister would read us a quick story and kiss us goodnight. I wished that my mammy would put me to bed but that was out of the question.

Bernard, too, had to go to bed at the same time as his baby brother. Because he was poorly and exhausted, he usually went straight to sleep. Often I would lie awake for what seemed like hours, on the right-hand side of Mammy's four-foot bed, running my eyes over the dingy floral wallpaper, the thick floral curtains. I was never good at nodding off, my young mind always too tense. I'd listen to the outside noises, like the hand-pushed lawnmowers and voices, yearning to go out and play. In winter, I would hear the TV and long to go down to see what was on. Sometimes, I'd sneak downstairs and peek at the TV through the crack in the living-room door, until eventually I felt sleepy.

Though toys were few and far between, I did have my little matchbox cars, which I worshipped. Since Daddy died, we hadn't had a real car, so I loved fantasising about driving down leafy lanes or going on holiday in my motor, me at the wheel, having wild and wonderful adventures.

It became commonplace for my older brother to take his frustration out on me – perhaps this was his way of venting his anger at the difficulties of his young life. But, in hindsight, it is apparent that we kids were desperately competing for any scrap of affection our mother threw at us. We craved attention from her, craved to be listened to, reassured and cared for. With nothing to unite us, as siblings we fell apart, and bullying behaviour became the norm for some.

I had no clear understanding of what was unfolding before me. Yet, on a very deep level, feelings of neglect, victimisation and a deep craving for attention were becoming deeply rooted in me and would play out drastically in the years to come.

4

Seen But Not Heard

1964 might have been the beginning of the hippy era, of free love and The Beatles, but in south-west Ireland, society was still tough, God-fearing and prudish. In 1960s' Ireland, the notion persisted that if you 'spared the rod, you spoiled the child'. Corporal punishment was condoned by the Church, and parents were not the only ones who were unenlightened about how to bring up their kids. Many a priest slapped me round the head during these early years in my childhood, and I witnessed nuns beat the living daylights out of their young charges. There was a culture of violence, which condoned my mother's increasingly unpredictable behaviour. It seemed that beatings for the slightest perceived wrongdoing were the norm, and I believed that this was normal behaviour in families. After all, what did I have to compare it with?

The atmosphere in our house remained tense. The two

years since my father and brother had died had been desperately difficult, and my mother still wasn't coping. She was still reeling from grief. Physical aggression was an outlet for her trauma.

As a small child, I was constantly in fear of Mammy's wrath. I never knew who was to get it next, or why. My earliest memory of being beaten is when I was around three years old and playing on my own in the back garden. I can't remember what I was supposed to have done. I was punished with a wooden spoon. I remember the red welts on my skin afterwards. I remember, too, the feelings of humiliation and confusion.

It's around this time that I began to 'escape' from home. My sisters often tell the story of my first 'runaway' attempt. The gate was open and, when no one was looking, I simply headed out of the house and out the gate, turning right. I passed the huge statue of Our Lady Queen of Peace at the triangle at the top of Marian Avenue, turned right and continued on my journey. Without getting run over, I managed to get myself as far as the Krupp's factory, which is a good mile away, up the Roxboro Road.

Once through the factory gates, I trundled around the shop-floor aisles, marvelling at the huge silvery machines that cranked and clunked all around me. The noise was deafening, the heat and light bewildering. I was fascinated by everything on the production line (Krupp's made household objects, like toasters and kettles) until I bumped into a pair of knees clad in denim overalls. A large creased face with big grey eyes came into view.

'And where do you think you're going?' a voice said.

My hand was gripped by a rough but firm hand, and the next thing I knew I was being marched through a door with glass panels at the top. Another man in a dark suit, who was speaking on a telephone, turned round, saw me and smiled in surprise: 'That child doesn't work here,' he said jovially.

'You might be right there,' said my keeper. They both guffawed. I was fascinated, taking in the office with its huge desk, charts and filing cabinets. It all seemed very strange and exciting, and certainly better than being at home. 'Aidan, would you take the little man back to his mammy?'

'I will indeed. Although the cat's got his tongue, it seems.' Both men looked at me, and I stared back, giving nothing away. I wanted my adventure to continue. I liked being away from home; here, people were nice to you. They talked to you – and gave you attention.

My nice man looked down at me and winked, and it felt good to know I wasn't in big trouble, whatever happened when I got home again. But there was no escaping the inevitable. I was whisked around and led out of the office and was soon perched on the handlebars of a rickety bicycle, which the man wheeled along. I hadn't been able to give him my exact address, but he asked around on the streets as to whether anyone knew who I belonged to. After a few enquiries, I was back on the doorstep of our house in Marian Avenue.

When the door opened, my mother dragged me inside. She punished me and ordered me to bed immediately. As I lay under the sheets, I felt utterly crestfallen that somehow my happy adventure had ended so badly. Deep down, I had hoped for a smile, a cuddle, an expression of relief that I had been returned safely. I'd seen her crying over my father, then my two brothers – and knew she was capable of feelings of love, and grief.

Later, Deirdre told me that my family had searched for me when they realised I was missing. The girls hunted through the trees and shrubs in the garden and called to neighbours' houses asking after me. My disappearance had caused a bit of a stir. But Mammy hadn't called the guards or got out a search party, the normal things you'd expect when a small child goes missing. She was probably too emotionally exhausted to deal with another family crisis. But this seeming lack of response registered in my young mind, and I wondered what it would take to make her care.

This type of behaviour on my part established a pattern. I would do anything to seek attention, despite any risk to my personal safety or health. I remember another episode, not long after, when I made a run for it. Again, I escaped through the open door and out the little wooden gate. I saw a bus coming and, when it stopped, I hopped on and hung onto the pole at the back. I made my way up the stairs, clambered onto a front seat and settled in for the journey. I recall sitting in the front seat, waving out at everyone. I even remember the bus passing my own front door, where my mother and a couple of my sisters stood, waving back. I'm not sure if they realised it was me.

What stands out in my memory is a feeling of immense freedom. Indeed, I see this particular episode as a formative experience. Even now, if the going gets tough, I feel this need to escape: to the sea, the countryside or even just by gazing at clouds.

On I journeyed, this time all the way over to a place called Ballynanty Beg, which is on the other side of Limerick City. Only at the last stop did the conductor realise he still had a little passenger who didn't belong to one of the grown-ups. Luckily, he took the time to bring me home to Janesboro.

Unsurprisingly, when I got home, there wasn't a welcoming committee. After Mammy exchanged some pleasantries with the bus driver and parted ways, the shit hit the fan. Pretty soon, all the sense of joy from my short escape was thoroughly knocked out of me.

At age four, I did get my chance to escape legitimately, and on a regular basis. It was time to start at Janesboro National School. I was excited at the prospect of school – being the youngest in the family, I had witnessed my sisters and, now, Bernard, heading out daily, and for me, starting school was a coming of age, an important milestone in my young life.

It was a relief to escape from the hardships of home. But trouble seemed to be constant in those early days, at home and, as it would turn out, in school. On one particular occasion, I was late, a not unusual event. By the time I arrived, all the children had gone inside. I hung around the playground for a time, pondering what to do. I felt caught between the Devil and the deep blue sea, as I feared the wrath of the teachers for being late but also feared the response from Mammy if I didn't attend at all.

I made a decision. I turned out of the school gate and ran away. I went to a favourite spot where I often played with friends from the street, 'Cal's Field', down by the railway line. This was a soccer pitch in the part of the city where the railway bridge went across from the Janesboro side to the Weston side.

Time passed, though I didn't know how much. I knew I'd be in big trouble if Mammy found out I wasn't in school. I was a highly anxious child, afraid of going home to face the inevitable. I watched the trains pass, hauling their loads down to the Irish Cement factory, and generally tried to stave off boredom. After what seemed like hours, I saw some schoolchildren passing and assumed it was the end of the school day. I set out for home.

As I proceeded up the road from Cal's Field to Janesboro, I saw Larry, a local man I knew. I liked Larry. He was a kind man who always had the time of day for me, and I had a fantasy that one day he would marry my mother and become my father. It didn't occur to me that he may have had his own wife and family. Larry was a corporation worker, and, on this particular day, he was walking along the road with his grey horse and cart.

I hopped on the back of his cart and enjoyed sitting in the straw. I passed people from the neighbourhood and saluted them grandly. As the horse plodded along slowly, Larry turned to me. 'And why aren't you at school?'

'School's out,' I said.

Larry said nothing more until we drew up alongside our house. Within what seemed like seconds, my mother was at the gate, looking angry. Larry had barely waved goodbye when she set to work. This time was particularly severe, as she came at me with her black leather belt. I was ordered into the small bathroom upstairs, and I recall being crouched on the floor, terrified, hands in front of my face, as I tried to stave off the belts. When she had finally vented her fury, she returned downstairs, leaving me huddled there on the floor, sobbing quietly.

That same day, there were some corporation workers cleaning out the gutters and replacing the eaves on the side of our house. Hearing the commotion, one of them tiptoed in through the open front door and crept upstairs. The concerned worker peeked his head around the bathroom door and surveyed my blotched face, the cuts and welts covering my arms and legs. He looked shocked. 'Are you OK, child?' he whispered.

Here was someone who could help. I looked at his kindly, weather-beaten face and wondered if I dare say anything. But

I was in enough trouble already. 'Yeah, I'm all right,' I whispered.

The man could obviously see I was in a bad way, and he looked anxiously over his shoulder down the stairs, to where Mammy had disappeared to the back of the house. 'Are you sure?' he whispered again.

It felt incredible that someone actually cared about me, and I wanted to jump up and plead with him to take me away. If only I could tell, the relief would be enormous. But I bit my lip. I knew what would really lie ahead if I gave the game away. The unspoken rule in our house was to keep quiet about what really went on behind closed doors, or risk your life.

'Yeah, I'm definitely sure,' I said. 'I did something wrong and my mother said I deserved some slaps for it.'

'But you're all marked,' the worker said softly.

'Yeah, this is nothing. I'll get over it. I always do,' I said.

The worker cast his eye over me one more time, shook his head wearily and disappeared from the bathroom door. I stood up silently and splashed water on my face, relieved that at least the ordeal was over.

I was put to bed unceremoniously that afternoon. I cried into the pillow and wondered, not for the first time, why things always seemed to end up this way in our unhappy house.

5

Robbing Peter to Pay Paul

Poverty creates its own pressures and, undoubtedly, part of my mother's anger must have been triggered by the stress and strain of having to single-handedly feed, clothe and school six children.

One memory that stands out from my early years was seeing *Oliver!*, the film of Charles Dickens' book *Oliver Twist*, on television one Sunday afternoon. It chimed with my life exactly. I identified with this poor, unloved blond boy, hungry and in rags, who was bossed around by everyone and who asked innocently enough for 'more' only to land himself in hot water. Indeed, secretly, I thought Oliver's life in a Victorian orphanage would be far preferable to living in our household.

During my early schooldays, I remember feeling embarrassed by my lack of clean clothes. I had one white shirt, which was permanently grey and frayed. I distinctly remember scrubbing the shirt and cuffs using a nailbrush and the dreaded carbolic soap a couple of times a week, then hanging it up, hoping against hope it would drip dry in time for the next day. Often in winter I went to school with it still wet. My sisters and, later, I usually did the family ironing.

For some reason, probably money, I didn't have a pair of the long grey woollen shorts to wear to school, as was customary for boys of my age. Instead, I was sent in 'shorter' black shorts, similar to football shorts. They exposed my white, skinny thighs and, naturally enough, the other kids teased me, giving me the humiliating nickname 'Underpants', which stuck with me for years. When, soon enough, my life was to take a serious downturn with the onset of sexual abuse, I believed that these shorts had something to do with it.

'Robbing Peter to pay Paul' was the norm for many impoverished families of that time. Mammy had to borrow the money for what clothes we had, from the United Dominians Trust or other agencies. The particular store where she shopped also offered loans to customers but at a high rate of interest. Looking back, they were like glorified moneylenders to the poor, and almost everyone around us used them, often getting deeper and deeper into debt. The store hired 'agents' to go out and collect the money every Saturday: their very own debt collectors.

One Saturday, when I was about six, I remember sitting on the kitchen floor playing with soldiers. It was a drizzly, dreary afternoon, and none of my friends were out on the street playing. When the ominous knock came on the front door, my heart sank. Mammy got up and tiptoed into the front room, then slowly moved back one curtain and lifted a slat of blind.

'It's him,' she whispered conspiratorially. 'Go out and tell him I'm not here . . . tell him I will be back next Saturday and that I will pay him on the double then.'

My heart sank a few more inches into my chest but I knew better than to argue. I left my soldiers and went into the hallway. I could see the shadow of the man through the glass. Mammy pushed me towards the door and I opened it, quivering, trying to remember her exact words. I'd be in trouble if I got it wrong. I peered up at a tall, formidable man in a raincoat, standing on our doorstep.

'Is your mammy at home?' he boomed down at me.

I blinked fast, desperately trying to remember my lines. I felt very small indeed in his shadow. 'Mammy says she isn't here but she told me to tell you that she would be here next week and that she will pay you on the double.' My voice got smaller and quieter as I delivered the message.

The man glared at me disbelievingly, then scribbled something down on his clipboard. After several weeks of this repeated performance, he got more and more fed up until, finally, one afternoon, he bent down and put his big face right up to mine. His eyes were bloodshot. 'You'd better tell your mother, when she gets back' – he raised his voice at this point for emphasis and stared pointedly at the parlour window – 'that if she's not here on the next occasion that I'm here, it's not knocking I'll be.'

I blinked at him, my bottom lip trembling. My heart was banging in my chest: I had no idea what this man was capable of doing. I went to Mammy and repeated to her, on demand, what had gone on. Once again, I became a vent for her frustration, as she reached for the belt.

Even in those early days, I was good at coming up with schemes. There may not have been many luxuries at home, but, if anything, that would make you all the more enterprising. One evening, when Mammy was out, myself and Bernard were at home feeling bored. 'Would you like to get a few sweets?' I asked.

'Yeah, that would be great, but we have no money,' said Bernard.

I thought for a minute. My tummy was rumbling and I felt a bit devilish. 'Well,' I said, 'we could always go around a few doors of our neighbours' houses and tell them we are collecting money for the Missions and then spend the money on ourselves.' I felt nervous even as I said the words, as it seemed like such an outlandish thing to do. But it was just idle talk – Bernard would never agree to it. And, sure enough . . .

'I will not do that,' he said, looking suitably shocked. 'I'm an altar boy and I will not have anybody saying that I collected money for the Missions and didn't give the money up.'

He was right. I was defeated. 'Suit yourself,' I said. I sat there for five more minutes, feeling frustrated. I wanted sweets. We rarely had any treats. I thought it through: I could just collect a penny or two from each house, so it wouldn't be a major crime or anything. I'd occasionally dipped into my mother's purse before now, and she'd seldom noticed a couple of pennies missing. I was very careful, because I knew a large amount would be noticed, and the consequences would be serious. I was convincing myself that my scam was justified, and suddenly felt utterly convinced of my cause.

'OK, I'm off,' I said bravely.

I explained my 'mission' for the Missions on quite a few doorsteps, to some surprising success, and then went running to the shop and bought a huge plastic bag full of penny toffee bars. On our return, I found, to my dismay, that Mammy was back. Immediately, the game was up. Knowing better than to argue, I quickly owned up.

Without delay, I was unceremoniously dragged to the living room, where trouble ensued. Needless to say, the fruits of my unholy labour – the sweets – were confiscated in front of my child's eyes. But it had been fun, working out my innocently devious plan, an early and never-to-be-forgotten jostle with the rules of wheeling and dealing.

Anyway, there were other ways of getting treats. We often got our groceries on 'tick' from a local corner shop. The sweet old lady grocer was a secret ally to us kids, and sometimes my sisters, my brother and I would get sweets, crisps, biscuits and chocolate, instead of the staples we had been told to get, such as ham, bread and cheese. She would write down the sensible things and wink at us conspiratorially. I think she somehow understood that we had to get our pleasure somewhere, and thankfully she was complicit in helping us.

I don't recall birthday parties when we were children. But Deirdre, who assumed much of the household respon-sibilities, did what she could to make such occasions memor-able, sometimes scrounging eggs to make a sponge cake, light as air, or some chocolate rice crispie buns. When, later, Deirdre left for England to train as a nurse, I would miss her enormously.

Similarly, Christmas was a low-key affair. Christmas lunch we ate alone – it was never an occasion that was shared with friends or family, or even neighbours.

Thankfully, Santa did come, though. We each had a stocking to hang up on the mantelpiece on Christmas Eve, and it would have some sweets in it the following morning. This was very exciting and a welcome respite from the drudge of every day. Sometimes we'd even have one present each. I might be lucky and get some more matchbox cars, or toy soldiers, or even new clothing of my very own, rather than the usual hand-me-downs.

I began to look forward to summer because our neighbours – the Crawfords on one side and the Sweeneys on the other – had apple trees. An orchard was a target for a schoolboy raid. The Crawfords were perfect for a raid, as they had a long shed that ran along under the trees. I'd walk along the top of the shed, taking care because it was quite tricky, and I could end up with my feet through the roof if I slipped. I'd come away with a bag of the delicious fruit, and Deirdre would make an apple pie after a raid. We'd happily munch on apples for weeks, with no real questions asked.

At other times, I was sent out by Mammy to pick up the coal that fell from the Tedcastle coal lorries as they left the Limerick docks. I would forage for nice big lumps and return home with a couple of plastic bagfuls to keep the family warm. It made me feel good, like a little provider.

One early morning, when I was seven years old, I woke up with a pain in my stomach. It was bad enough for my mother to call the doctor and, as the day progressed, it intensified. As we waited for his arrival, the pain became severe, and my mother grew increasingly anxious. Twelve hours passed with no sign of him before she decided to take the matter into her own hands. A helpful neighbour, Mrs Kennedy, who had a car, drove me to the hospital. Once there, I was quickly prepared for an emergency operation; I had developed appendicitis, and the long delay while we waited for the doctor had resulted in my appendix bursting.

Only for Mrs Kennedy's kindness and the fact that she had a car at her disposal, it is possible I would have died. As a result of the ruptured appendix, peritonitis had set in and I was critically ill. I've very little memory of the procedure that followed or the level of anxiety surrounding me. All I recall is the swirling blackness as I went under the anaesthetic and, after the operation, the slow, sickening recovery to consciousness.

But I was a young boy, healthy and strong, apart from this setback, and my recovery was swift. I enjoyed the food, in particular the nightly jelly and ice cream. I had a regular supply of my favourite comics, and the nurses were kind to me. I recovered quickly in this regulated, clean environment and soon made friends with a couple of the other boys in the ward, who, like me, enjoyed getting up to mischief.

As my condition improved, restlessness set in, and we started to get up to no good. One morning, the three of us snuck out of the ward, past the duty sister and onto the main corridor outside. We reached the lift and, checking that no one was looking, we pressed the button. It rattled to life and began creaking towards us. We stood there, in our hospital dressing gowns, barefoot and giggling. In my mind, I was James Bond, as I stepped into the lift and shut the door behind me.

I hit the down button, and we shot down to the basement. I pressed the up button, and up we went again. Then one of the boys pressed down, and down we shot. The craic was ninety, and we laughed our heads off, riding the lift up, then down until, suddenly, we saw her.

A grim-set face appeared through the glass in the door. It belonged to a nun, and one glance at her expression told us that she was absolutely furious. Trouble was in store. She had caught the culprits red-handed, and her eyes held an unnerving glint of triumph. Quick as a flash, I stabbed at the button as she lunged at the door and grabbed the outside handle. She tugged hard, trying to force it open. On the other side, we were equally determined to keep it closed. My new-found friend held fast, pulling with all his might onto the handle on our side. He was helped by the second boy and myself. We hung on to him for dear life and pulled as hard as we could.

It was a comic tug of war, but the nun was winning out, in spite of our best efforts. I kept stabbing furiously at the lift button with my free hand and, suddenly, it sprung into life. Slowly it began to journey upwards. I watched through the door window as the nun sank away beneath us. But she wasn't going to be so easily defeated.

I saw her break for the stairwell as the floor disappeared from sight. Then, just as we got to the first floor, she came flying towards us, florid-faced and furious. Just as she reached the lift, I hit the button hard, and up we shot again. She was almost ahead of us when we arrived at the second floor, and she lunged towards the door handle again, but my timing was getting good and, right on cue, I hit the down button.

The game was on. We went up and down, hotly pursued by our angry nun, until we finally won the battle. Defeated and exhausted, she had to quit the chase. We eventually stumbled back to our beds with tears of mirth streaming down our faces. It was one of the few situations I can remember when I actually got the better of an adult and, boy, did I enjoy the experience.

Soon, I was back home and, no longer cosseted as an invalid, life continued as usual. I was constantly on the watch for the slightest sign that Mammy was angry and often failed to dodge her wrath. I was still a very anxious child, often trying hard to suppress feelings of jitteriness and fear, and I ritually used cheekiness at school as a defence against these feelings.

I also took risks on the street, especially with other people's property. I learned to 'borrow' things if they were left unlocked, like bikes at school. My friend Eugene Geary had a 'Chopper' bike. These were all the rage at the time, and he would lend it to me for a ride down the street. It didn't have brakes, so I ended up on my rear end the first time I tried it out. Our gang would head out on bikes – mine was always borrowed – to Curragh Chase, a beautiful little forest outside the city. We had great adventures creating our own treasure trails through the woods. We'd also go fishing for eels and had many a summer's evening out at the Chase, playing typical boys' games. I never told my mother, as she was understandably worried about me cycling, after Declan's death. I spent as much time as I could out of the house but, as ever, seven o'clock was bedtime, whatever the season. And woe betide you if you were not in bed by then.

My First Holy Communion day was special, a rare happy event which we celebrated with our extended family. I was thrilled to be the centre of attention. I'd received the Blessed Sacrament for the first time and enjoyed the money that came my way from my relations. My uncle Jim, my mother's brother for whom I'd often run errands and deliver shoes, was especially generous.

Although I was warned not to smoke, it wasn't long before I was puffing away in secret. Smoking was a sign of sophistication. It made me one of the gang and that was more powerful to a little boy than any dire threats. I had my first cigarette once I got to primary school and would often smoke with the other boys behind the bike sheds or out in the woods, when we went out on bikes. It was part of the camaraderie.

In any case, in the 1960s, there was little public awareness that smoking could kill. It was possible to buy cigarettes in ones or twos with just a few pence. My mother was still a smoker but, despite the fact that we were often sent to the shops to buy cigarettes for her, we would have been punished for smoking ourselves. Mammy was doing her best against the odds to control her family, but we found our own ways of escaping from her strict regime, and this secretive act was one of mine. I was an asthmatic, so it was obviously a nonsense for me to smoke but, whenever I had a few pennies to spare, I'd afford myself this treat. It got rid of the constant nagging sensation of anxiety.

As I got older, my behaviour became more challenging, as the effects of my difficult young life began to take hold. On the street, I was quick to join gangs but, despite trying to flex my muscles, I was actually quite an effeminate child. I had fair hair and a slender body and bore a striking resemblance to my brother Declan.

I'd never known a father figure, but that didn't mean I didn't miss having a father. There were times when I met dads in other families and I realised what I was missing out on. I remember one family on our road, the Conroys, had a wonderful father. Mr Conroy used to fix the electrics up at the church. I remember going up to help him when I was around eight, handing him cables or passing up various tools to him. He treated his children well, giving them sweets on an equal basis, and I was in awe of him.

Mr Conroy used to bundle myself and Bernard into the back of his car, with his own brood, and take us for long spins out to Shannon Airport, where we'd look at the planes. These were magic moments. The airport had a nostalgic resonance with my own father, and my trips here with Mr Conroy gave me a wonderful taste of what it would have been like to have a father who would help me to learn about the world.

As for my mother, tired from the endless grind of work and the chaos of home, she decided one day that she'd had enough and taught us a lesson we would never forget.

6

The Disappearance

One morning, I woke up to a house that had an altogether different atmosphere than usual. Even from upstairs in my bedroom I sensed it. I heard laughter, and the sound of the television, which was never usually allowed on before we went to school.

When I came down and entered the kitchen, the mood was giddy. My sisters helped themselves to food from the fridge, banged doors and made no effort to be quiet so that our mother could rest. Mammy was nowhere to be seen. She was not in the bedroom or the bathroom. Nor could I see her hanging clothes out on the line. Where was she? Sensing my confusion, Sorcha bent down and explained that Mammy had gone away.

I had no idea what she meant. My mother had never gone away. She worked and came home, and even when she was in a bleak humour, I always knew she was near. What exactly did 'gone away' mean? Daddy and Declan had gone away. I understood that kind of parting, but this, I knew, was different.

Everyone seemed quite happy, which meant it couldn't be too serious. In his new-found liberation, Bernard decided he wouldn't go to school, and I quickly jumped on the bandwagon. But order had not vanished completely, and my older sisters insisted we did. Soon, we trundled off on our way.

I fully expected Mammy to be home again when I returned from school that afternoon. To my surprise, there was still no sign of her. To all intents and purposes, she had disappeared into thin air. The afternoon turned to evening and then to night. We helped ourselves to food out of the fridge and stayed up late watching TV. An air of anarchy had developed in the house. It felt weird and wonderful to do exactly what we wanted. But the worry was never far away. Shouldn't we tell someone our mother was missing – the police or a teacher, the local priest? But no one seemed inclined to do anything about her disappearance.

Eventually, Sorcha explained that a huge row had occurred between Mammy and the older girls. Sorcha didn't elaborate on what triggered it, but the resulting storm was enough to make Mammy's mind up. She packed a bag and headed out the door, claiming she was fed up looking after us. She was going to 'run away' just like we ran away from time to time (I wasn't the only one to slip out of the house for some freedom whenever I could).

It seemed that she had taken off to Dublin, leaving the older girls in charge. Sorcha was eighteen at the time. We went to bed that night without hearing from her. No word came through the next day, not a phone-call, nothing. Life went on. My older sisters went out with their boyfriends, and Deirdre assumed the role of mother as best she could. Needless to say, it didn't take long for the excitement of our new-found liberation to wear off. After a few days, food stocks began to run low. We had no access whatsoever to money. By the time Friday came around, there was nothing except a few rashers and sausages left in the fridge.

It was customary for Catholics to abstain from meat on Friday, and we usually ate fish for our main meal. Not this Friday. We were absolutely starving and had no money to buy fish. As the day wore on, hunger began to overcome the fear of committing a sin. With the knowledge that we were probably ruining our chances of heaven, we all agreed: there was nothing for it but to tuck into a dinner of rashers and sausages.

A day later, my mother reappeared. No hugs or kisses were exchanged. She offered no explanation for her long absence, and I was afraid to ask in case she disappeared again. As she took off her coat, she said, 'Now you know what it's like without me and, if I hear any more arguments, I will run away again and, next time, I won't come back.'

Impulsively, probably in a bid to get her attention, I piped up: 'Mammy, there is one thing you should know, they gave us meat yesterday.'

With that, all hell broke loose. She shouted at the girls, who shouted back. Life in the Devane household had returned to normal.

This episode would mark a sea change in my mother's behaviour. I later discovered that her trip to Dublin had acquainted her with the city's pub life. She had left to escape from the pressures of family life and perhaps she had discovered that drinking in a pub was a good way to forget everything. I'm sure she had found solace not only in the drink but in grown-up company too – after all, she was still a relatively young woman, only in her late thirties, and must have felt lonely for adult company.

From the time I was seven, she had occasionally sent me to buy two pint bottles of Guinness for her and would reward me afterwards with a small glass. This was a weekly ritual, which went with the Sunday roast, cooked at first by Mammy and Deirdre, and later by Deirdre alone. Then Mammy began to drink little quarter bottles of 'Black and White' whiskey, termed a 'naggan', and again I was sent up to the shop to fetch one or two for her.

After Mammy's trip to Dublin, her taste developed for beer and whiskey on a regular basis. This drinking habit would, in time, be passed on to me. I'd tasted alcohol for the first time when I was four when she allowed me to drink a small glass of

Guinness, dark and bitter, like drinking medicine, but I liked the heady, dizzy feeling I got from it. As I grew older, it would become my main means of blotting out the painful emotions of life.

By the age of eight, I had become a vulnerable child, needy and easily lured by anything that seemed to offer comfort or gain. I found it hard to trust people or disclose things when I needed to. Deep down I felt that I was an undeserving child, different to other, more contented, children I saw around me. As a result, my behaviour could often be secretive and devious. In short, I had become an easy target. But nothing that had gone before prepared me for the dangerous downward path that now awaited me.

7

The End of Innocence

By the time I was eight years old, my mother had begun working during the day as a registrar at St Camillus's hospital, registering births, marriages and deaths. She was still doing some night shifts as a telephonist at St Munchin's. At home, we'd often crowd upstairs in the top front bedroom, watching through the curtains for her return. As soon as she came round the corner into Marian Avenue, we would discern from her face what kind of mood she was in. Often, the signs were not good. Her routine was to come home, make a cup of tea, light a cigarette and go into the back living room to watch TV.

I learned to keep out of her way. One sunny afternoon during the summer, I was outside kicking a ball with the other boys from the neighbourhood. Mammy had arrived home half an hour earlier. It was obvious from her expression that she was not in good humour. I made myself scarce, hoping that by the time I got back from soccer her mood would have improved. There were eight of us, a stocky, tough-looking bunch, ranging in age from about eight to ten. We always used Mrs Fahey's gates, near our house, as one set of goal posts, and Mr McCann's gates, a bit up the road, as the other.

As usual, I was wearing my one and only pair of small black shorts. They were the bane of my life and, as the other boys wore the standard long grey ones that went down to their knees, I imagine I must have stood out a bit from the gang.

Ours was a large and busy neighbourhood, and we knew lots of people by sight, but didn't necessarily know them personally. One such person was a young man in his early twenties, named Aidan for the purposes of this story. That evening, he ambled up the street and stood on the pavement for a few moments, watching us play. No one paid any attention to him as my friend Chris fired the ball for our team between Mr McCann's goalposts. Score! We jumped up and down and punched the air.

We broke for half-time. As we loitered, chatting around the gate pillars, I noticed Aidan watching me intently. He looked anxious. I wondered if he was in trouble. He beckoned to me. I didn't want to leave the game, but we were on a break, and his look was urgent.

Aidan was around twenty-three, unshaven with wispy dark hair. I think he was unemployed and still living at home with his parents. I'd never spoken to him before, despite having seen him plenty of times around the neighbourhood.

He lived a few streets away; indeed, his younger brother often kicked a ball about with us. He always looked a bit down at heel, and I imagined he was something of a loner, but then most people on our street were struggling, and who was I to judge? Besides, I knew better than to cross an adult.

Panting from the game, I walked over to where he stood and waited to hear what he had to say. He leaned down and whispered to me, 'It's John, isn't it?'

I nodded, still catching my breath. I could hear the boys beginning to kick the ball behind me again and was eager to get back to the game. To myself, I urged him to get on with it.

'The thing is, I'm doing wallpapering and stuff for my mother and father, you know, and I need somebody to help me finish it off, I'll give you fifty pence for it.'

Fifty pence! My eyes widened at the thought. I was astounded. Fifty pence was a lot of money in my world: it could buy an ocean of sweets and cigarettes. I could get ten No.6 for ten pence at that time, and often did. At this stage, I was regularly stealing my mother's or a sister's cigarettes and was enjoying my secret habit down the garden or under a friend's shrubs.

I turned briefly and looked at the lads, who were back stuck into the match. Chris looked over at me and waved his arm in irritation, signalling to me to come back and join in. I looked at Chris, then back at Aidan. I felt torn, but only momentarily. I wanted to go on playing soccer, but fifty pence! I observed Aidan's anxious face, which had beads of sweat breaking out on it. He looked really worried, so I figured he was anxious to finish the job.

'It won't take long,' he said, as if reading my mind.

My decision was made. I'd earn my fifty pence and be back in the game in no time – a rich man! I shouted over to the lads, 'I'll see you in a bit.'

A few of the boys glanced in my direction and Chris shouted, 'Good luck.'

I was trotting down the road next to Aidan. I'd never spoken to him before, and an awkward silence fell between us. We reached his house in a couple of minutes. It was exactly the same as my own house, and just as run down.

Aidan opened the front door and we went inside. His parents weren't there. I stood in the hall for a moment, and Aidan gestured towards the door on the left, the same as our front parlour at home. In fact, the whole house looked like my own, expect there were more holy pictures on display.

'It's in here,' he said. He went to the door and opened it. I followed and walked into the middle of the room, facing the tiled fireplace, but was instantly confused. Had we entered the wrong room? There was no sign of any decorating, not a single paintbrush or can of paint in sight.

I turned around to ask Aidan where the paint was and saw him locking the door. He took the key out of the lock and put it in his trouser pocket. 'I didn't bring you down for decorating after all,' he said mysteriously. 'It's OK.'

I felt a slight pang of discomfort, but dismissed it. He must want me to move some furniture, or roll up the carpet. I looked around the dingy room, which was definitely in need of a lick of paint. So what was the job then? I looked back at Aidan and he moved towards me. I could suddenly smell the unwashed stench of his armpits.

In a flash, I knew I was in danger. My eyes darted to the windows. They were closed. The door was locked. I was completely trapped. I edged backwards towards the fireplace, by now very frightened. My instinct was to run, and my eyes darted either side of Aidan, assessing my means of escape. But he read my mind and hastened towards me. 'I didn't bring you here to decorate . . .' he said. Aidan was openly sweating now and had a strange, glazed look in his eyes. I'd never seen such a look before, and I didn't like it. 'Lie down,' he said.

'What?'

He moved closer, nearly touching me now. I could smell his bad breath. His teeth were heavily discoloured. He towered over me. In answer to my question, he put his hands on my shoulders and pushed me down towards the floor. 'I want you to lie down.'

Intimidated, I did as told. I heard a clock ticking somewhere, and birdsong in the garden outside. Aidan was still looking very anxious. He suddenly knelt down next to me, on my right side. Though I felt a chilling sense of menace, I still had no idea what was happening.

Throughout the invasion that followed, I was unable to speak. Not one word did I utter from when he first placed his hand down my pants to when the whole, sordid ordeal was over. The more agitated he became, the more frightened I grew. I had never ever touched myself there, except for going to the toilet or washing.

As he masturbated himself and invaded my private parts, a sense of revulsion rose up in me. I prayed that whatever was happening would stop. I kept looking into his face for any clues. To me, he had turned into a monster, grimacing, with his broken black teeth like a nasty Incredible Hulk.

Aidan forced me to turn over, and I remember the burn of the maroon carpet on my face. Then the weight of his enormous bulk crushed down on my back. I remember his stinking breath as I struggled to breathe. There was no way of moving free.

I remember the sensation of something hard between my legs, like a stick or a piece of wood. It was moving up and down, pressing onto my body, rubbing against me. I tried to move my head to one side, to breathe easier, but I couldn't. I wondered whether my body could take his weight for much longer without my chest caving in. I glanced sideways at him again and saw his screwed-up face.

I felt myself floating up, out of my body, witnessing what was happening to me as if from afar. In this detached state, I wondered how I had got myself into this situation. And when it would be over.

Suddenly, I felt something pulsing between my legs. A foul smell, like rotten fish, hit my nostrils. I wanted to cry, I wanted to scream, I wanted to run. But instead I stayed very still. I was in his power, and he knew it.

Now he was wiping me and removing what looked like watery cream from my private parts. I felt completely exposed. He sat down on the sofa. Suddenly, there was the sound of a key turning in the front door. Aidan's expression quickly changed from one of calm self-satisfaction to horror, and he raised his finger up to his lips.

'Get up!' he hissed.

I sat up, blinking, and noticed a wet patch on the carpet, where my body had lain moments before. Aidan grabbed my shorts from round my ankles and yanked them up, unceremoniously. By now I was totally dazed. I heard voices in the hall: his parents. A jolt of fear ran through me. Did they know what was happening in their parlour? Should I tell them or would I be in trouble? I suddenly imagined the adults coming in and shouting at me about what was going on in their house.

Meanwhile, Aidan was panicking. He rushed to the window and threw it open. There was a large privet hedge between the house and the road, screening the parlour from view. I was pushed unceremoniously out the window and found myself on the ground. A fifty-pence piece landed on the dirt next to me. 'There's your money,' he said from the open window.

I picked up the coin and put it in my pocket. Stunned, I rose to my feet. Aidan leaned further out the window and grabbed my shirt. He pulled me roughly up to his face. He was still sweating, although his complexion was not so red now. 'Don't tell anybody about this. No one will believe you if you do. I'll tell them it was all your fault if you say a word to anyone. And then I will kill you and I'll kill your mother too. D'you hear? If you tell your mother about this, I will kill you.' And with that the window was slammed shut and Aidan was gone.

I scrambled to my feet, my heart racing, and began to run. It was a relief to run, but where would I go? As I rounded the corner, I saw the boys still kicking the ball. It seemed a lifetime ago since I had left them. In the blink of an eye, my whole life, my whole universe, had changed. I was not the same child that went willingly down the road less than half an hour ago, to earn fifty pence for a spot of decorating. I was a different child, almost an alien, coming back from a faraway land, with a heavy coin in my pocket.

I stood on the pavement near my house and watched the boys play, unable to bring myself to join in. My knees were shaking, my stomach heaving. I wanted to tell them, but how could I? What words would I use? They might laugh when I tried to explain what had happened. Besides, how could I explain what I did not understand myself? I felt almost faint with fear and desperately tried to hold back tears.

Chris looked up at me briefly. 'How come you finished so quickly?'

Go on, tell him, I thought. But I didn't know what to say. At last I found my voice. I tried hard to sound casual when I felt as if I had been turned inside out by some external force. 'Oh, he just needed a hand for a few minutes.'

How ironic was that? A hand. For a few minutes. Embarrassed, I turned away and walked to the shop. I put my fifty pence on the counter and asked for a pack of ten No. 6. I took the cigarettes and ran. I found a bush on a bit of scrub land and smoked three cigarettes, one after the other. Although I felt sick, I also felt a brief comfort from the heady lightness that filled my brain.

I tried to make sense of what had happened. I must have done something to deserve it. Punishment was usually deserved for doing something bad, even if I was not always sure exactly what that bad thing was.

My racing mind fixed on an earlier memory, of a beating I'd received once in school, from a nun called Sister Pious. It wasn't the first time I'd been slapped, but this was different, and I'd never been able to forget the humiliation of that experience. I was a junior pupil at Janesboro Primary School. Sister Pious was an extremely strict teacher, a nun whose reputation for punishment was fearsome. On this particular morning, all the children were sitting at their desks as she wrote on blackboard, her back turned to the class.

Driven by a desire for attention, or perhaps just out of sheer childhood boldness, I stood on my chair and pulled down my pants. As the class erupted into laughter, I 'mooned' my little bare bottom at the nun. She swung around rapidly, just as I was pulling up my pants.

'John Devane!' she shrieked and strode furiously towards my desk. She peered down at me from under her crisp veil. Staring down at me from her hard black eyes, I was pinned to the chair in terror. She leaned forward and grabbed me by the right earlobe. My eyes watered as I yelped, all signs of bravado instantly disappearing.

She pulled me to my feet by my ear. It felt like it might become detached in her grip as she led me to the front of the class. I was ordered to stand with my hands behind my back as she went to her wooden cupboard and got out a black leather strap, which looked like a two-inch thick belt without a buckle.

'So you want to bare yourself to the class, do you?' She strode towards me menacingly. 'Drop your pants.'

That morning, I had worn a pair of my older brother's greyish, frayed pants. I looked at her appalled, unable to believe what I had heard.

'I said, drop your pants!' she repeated and swung me round, so my back was to the class. She then proceeded to pull the pants down to my knees. I was horrified by the realisation that the whole class was now watching my humiliation as I was forced to bend over, there and then. My bare bottom was exposed to the class, my pants round my ankles. You could hear a pin drop, as my classmates witnessed for the first time what would happen to them if they ever pulled such a trick.

Whack! The pain was excruciating. Tears sprung to my eyes, and I bit my lip as the first blow cracked across my skin. I dug my fingers into my knees to stop myself crying out and stared hard at the bare floorboards. She gave me ten of her very best and told me to pull up my pants and report to her office, as she was also head of the junior infants school. Tears were now streaming down my face. But worse was to come. I was forced to stand outside the office door until Mammy arrived at the school. Once inside her office, Sister Pious impressed on my unusually meek and polite mother the need for my total obedience. My terrible behaviour was beyond the bounds of what they would tolerate.

As we left his office, my mother's face was like thunder. She dragged me home roughly. Once inside our living room, I knew I was really in for it now. So it often was in those days – if you were beaten in school, there was good reason, and you would get it at home, too.

Would the same happen again now? As I smoked in the shelter of the bushes, I tried to control my trembling body and calm myself down enough to go home. I tried to convince myself that what had occurred in that dingy room had taken place in my imagination. Perhaps I was in the middle of a nightmare and when I woke up everything would be the same as before.

But I couldn't fool myself. This was not a dream that would fall away from me as I ran into a new day. No matter how many cigarettes I smoked, no matter how much I argued it in my mind, or wondered if it was some kind of sick game that grown-ups played, something disgusting had happened and, in some way, I was to blame. I was the guilty one. Otherwise, why would he have picked me out from the other boys? He must have known I was the only one who would go with him.

In my confused state, I imagined that *Aidan* would tell on *me*. At that thought, I began to sweat. If Mammy found out, I would be in big trouble, and that would mean a severe beating.

As I took slow, faltering steps home in the evening gloom, these thoughts swirled around my head. It was later than usual when I reached our doorstep. I stood there, wondering if I should knock on the door. I might have grown another head by now, I felt so different. Did I look different? Smell different?

I rang the bell and waited. My mother opened the door, turned and walked back down the hall. Obviously, I still looked like the same boy who had left the house earlier that afternoon, yet I felt as if I had aged a hundred years. I sat on the bottom of the stairs and listened to family life going on around me. Mammy was in the back living room, watching TV. The volume was loud, and I could hear the bursts of canned laughter from some comedy show. Grainne was washing clothes in the kitchen. Bernard was doing homework in the parlour.

I wanted to tell, but how? Aidan had said he'd say it was my fault, that I'd done it. Would my mother believe me, or him? I sat on the stairs for what seemed like an age until there was a break on TV and my mother went into the kitchen for a cup of tea. I'd missed supper, but I wasn't hungry. I still felt sick and was quaking uncontrollably inside.

Rolling up all my courage into a tight ball, I went into the kitchen and stood by the door, peeking around. I watched her fill the kettle and put it on to boil. I finally got up the courage to speak.

'Mammy.' My voice sounded tiny and insignificant. She didn't turn round. I went across the kitchen. She lifted a mug and placed a teabag in it.

'Mammy,' I said again, louder this time. 'You know Aidan over the road . . .' I gave his full name. She continued to make her tea, not turning round. 'Well, he brought me to his home . . . and he touched me . . .'

I felt the sudden slap of her hand across my face. 'You're a wicked child to say such a thing,' she said. 'Good neighbours do not do that sort of thing.'

I held my stinging face, shocked. The tears I had been barely holding back now began to flow uncontrollably. Mammy pushed past me with her mug of tea and went back into the living room without a backward glance, closing the door behind her.

The closed door spoke volumes. I stared at it for a moment, still crying silently. Finally, I dragged myself along the hall and up the stairs to the bathroom. Once inside, I pushed a chair up against the keyless door and took out the carbolic soap and nail brush. I undressed and began to scrub myself clean. I scrubbed my private parts, my legs, anywhere I could, trying to rid my body of Aidan's awful stench.

Eventually, worn out, I crawled into my bed and pulled the sheet over my head. I realised that there was no sense trying to talk to anyone about this thing that had taken place. I thought back to the other times when I had been punished. What had happened today was different. I understood enough to appreciate that difference, but there were similarities. The feeling of exposure and humiliation when my pants were pulled down, my flesh bared and damaged. The lack of power that came with being a small child. The awful knowledge that I had no control over what could happen to me at a moment's notice.

Yet, I also knew that, despite the similarities, this afternoon was different. The other times, no matter how painful the punishment, had a framework. You understood that if you misbehaved you were beaten. I remembered my classmates watching as I was beaten by the nun, knowing that they could just as easily be the one in the same situation if they also got into trouble. Being punished was a collective experience. But this . . . this set me apart from everyone I knew. They were clean. I was dirty. No amount of carbolic soap could get rid of that man's smell. Nothing could banish the scene that took place, silence the sounds, rid my body of his touch.

My thoughts raced feverishly around my head, jumbled

and incoherent as I tried to make sense of the afternoon. I cried silently into my pillow, aware that even my own mother didn't believe such things could happen. Or, worse still, she just did not believe me when I went to her for help. My small heart was broken. When the sun went down that day, my innocence went down with it.

8

Cat and Mouse Game

I was an altar boy, and served mass regularly, if often reluctantly, in the big Church of Our Lady Queen of Peace, at the top of our road. To all outward appearances, I was a normal child doing what was expected of me in what was perceived to be a protective Catholic environment. Sex was a no-no word. I didn't yet possess any serious sexual feelings and had never even played 'sexy' pretend games with other children. I'd never had any proper instruction about sex, either at home or at school, which was quite normal for that time.

Sex education was what you picked up along the way from friends or overheard in the playground. I'd heard about one young lad who was caught masturbating – known colloquially as 'fiddling with himself' – and, after being beaten for his mis-deed, he was brought to see a psychiatrist. The medical solution was to prescribe tranquillisers! I'm not sure they did any good, but the message was clear: 'fiddling with yourself' was wicked enough to warrant a visit to a shrink.

I'd shared one innocent kiss with Mary, a little girl from the neighbourhood, when we were playing together in her garden. We pressed our lips together briefly, keeping them tightly closed, and hugged each other. It was sweet and fun and made us giggle. However, her mother saw us, and I was sent packing. When I got home, she had called my mother and told her about my misdemeanour. Needless to say, this went down like a lead balloon but, despite the punishment meted out, I was excited by the idea that I had had my first kiss with someone who liked me, even if the grown-ups didn't approve.

Apart from that innocent experience, I knew little or nothing about the mechanics of sex or its emotional impact. Then Aidan happened and, after that first horrifying experience, my behaviour changed significantly; my knowledge was gained from bitter first-hand experience.

I was afraid to leave my house for fear of meeting him again. Once, outside my front door, I sensed I was in danger. Going to and from school, I constantly looked over my shoulder, fearing he might pounce on me. I felt haunted on my own street, on the bus, even in bed at night. I found it harder than ever to go to sleep. After school, instead of going out to kick a ball in the street with the lads, I stayed indoors. Whenever Chris called for me to come out, I'd shrug or shout back, 'Not today.' I isolated myself, fearing I would let something slip. If I blurted it all out to Chris while we were playing, what would happen then? The threat of being killed, or my mother being killed by my abuser, hung over me at all times.

I had one comfort. Bawneen, my beautiful white cat, became my only confidante. She listened patiently as I poured out my fears and woes into her furry little ears. I would distract myself by teasing her with strands of wool and stroking her soft fur, often for hours.

I was on the local soccer team and, after missing a few weeks, I braced myself and returned to play. I didn't want to let the team down and, besides, I loved the game. I was a good player, skilled with the ball, and loved being part of a team. It also helped keep my mind off my troubles. Once the game began and the adrenaline flowed, it was impossible to think about anything else.

A fire at a cardboard-box factory a few streets away also proved to be a welcome distraction. When the fire service arrived, I ran behind it to see what was going on. When the excitement was over and the fire quenched, I climbed aboard a Green Goddess. The firefighters let me sit in the driver's seat. I was allowed ring the bell. It was one of the most exciting moments of my young life and filled me with determination to be a firefighter when I grew up.

I was coming to the end of my time at Janesboro Primary School. It had brought me up to my holy commurnion, and soon I was to make the transition to my next school, the

Christian Brothers primary school in Sexton Street, Limerick. What should have been a summer of innocent exploration and simple enjoyment had been turned into something altogether more serious. I should have felt free to go down to the river to fish or to hang out with my friends, bagging apples. Instead, I felt haunted and afraid, like a hunted animal.

My life had become split into 'before Aidan' and 'after Aidan'. Before Aidan hadn't been the happiest of times, but after Aidan was beyond anything I'd ever imagined.

In the autumn of 1970, I started attending 'big school'. I would attend the Christian Brothers until I was thirteen. It felt good to be starting afresh. I was wearing Bernard's hand-me-down clothes but, at last, I had my first pair of longer grey shorts, along with one blue shirt and a blazer. I was very pleased with myself. In my young mind, I associated the shorter black 'underpants' shorts with what had happened to me with Aidan, believing that they were in some way responsible for making him choose me above the other boys. These longer shorts might offer some protection against such a dreadful thing happening again in the future.

Perhaps I could put it behind me. Perhaps Aidan had forgotten all about me and would never bother me again. The worst thing imaginable had happened to me, and I hoped it would only happen once.

Home was the usual chaotic place, but my older sisters were now beginning to move out, to work away from home or to train in various careers. They were interested in clothes, boys and going out at night – all the typical teenage stuff. They squabbled, fought and giggled together, and it was often a 'free-for-all' at home.

Deirdre, in the middle of us all, continued to be the one to 'mother' me the most. I wasn't a great reader, or great at drawing but, when she could, Deirdre spent time with me, helping with my homework, talking to me, telling me stories, taking care of me. And putting me to bed most nights, too.

But home wasn't a pleasant place to be, despite Deirdre's best efforts. I was a fearful and anxious child, always feeling unsettled, and my illicit smokes down the end of the back garden were my lifeline, the only thing that helped to calm my nerves. The skies could have been blue and the sun always shining, but I wouldn't have noticed.

One afternoon in that first week at my new school, I wandered home alone, satchel on my shoulder, humming to myself and feeling relatively carefree. On my way home, I had to cross over two railway bridges. The first, with timber walls, passed over the feeder line to the cement factory in Mungret, while the second, an attractive stone hump-backed bridge, went over the main passenger line. I was halfway across the second bridge when a red Escort drew up across the road from me. On seeing who was at the wheel, I stopped dead in my tracks, rigid with fear. The window rolled down, and Aidan shouted over to me. 'John. C'mere will you?'

I was rooted to the spot. I stared at the car, at Aidan, and tried to think what to do. If I ran straight ahead, he could catch up with me and cut me off; if I ran back, he could swing round and get me at the other end of the bridge. It was broad daylight, and I was conscious of people passing by. I didn't want to draw attention to myself.

'John!' Aidan's voice sounded sterner now. It was a command and, suddenly, I felt utterly trapped, like someone had put a ton weight on my chest. 'Get over here.'

Like an animal in a cage, I was powerless. Reluctantly, helplessly, my heart in my mouth, I obeyed. My mind seemed to be detached from my body, my legs moving of their own accord as I made my way towards the car. When I got there, Aidan was all smiles, like nothing at all out of the ordinary was happening. 'How are you, John? Why don't you get in the car?'

What did he mean? I didn't want to get in the car. My eyes darted down the bridge one way, then the other. I needed to run, to get out of there, but I was under the hypnotic hold of this strange man. The secret we shared repulsed me yet tied me to him, in some bizarre, twisted way.

'I'll take you home. Hop in.' He sounded benign but I instantly felt ensnared and vulnerable. All my life, grown-ups had told me what to do and I'd obeyed them.

'Get in the fuckin' car.' Not so benign after all, and the edge was back in his voice. The voice of a grown-up who would mete out punishment if you did not do what you were told. I went round to the other side of the car, convinced myself, however stupid it seemed, that he might want to apologise or make up for what had happened. No sooner had I sat down than I realised I'd made a big mistake. His smile disappeared when he reached over and pushed the button down on the passenger door, locking it. I felt instantly queasy. I placed my satchel between my thighs. Once again, I was under the control of an adult who had no idea what the word 'sorry' meant.

I stared out at the road, my hands shaking in my lap. Aidan drove on in silence. I didn't know where we were going. My mind was racing: He thinks I've told my mother, and he's going to kill me. This is the end. As we drove on, I became convinced that he was taking me to the river to drown me or someplace remote to strangle me. I had no idea what he was capable of.

Eventually, I recognised where we were. He was taking a shortcut to his house. I felt utterly desolate and terrified. What was I doing here, and how would I get away? Behind Aidan's house there were long fields, and it crossed my mind he might be thinking of burying me there. The stench of his sweat and breath hung heavy in the car, and my stomach heaved. The stark reality of our last meeting was clear in every detail. I clutched the handle of my schoolbag, willing the car to stop so that I could jump out and make a run for it.

The street was empty as we drew up to his house. Aidan got out of the car, walked around to my door and quickly unlocked it. 'Get out of the car,' he snapped nervously and gestured for me to go into the house.

I looked up at him, silently imploring him to let me go and wondered whether to run for it. He placed his heavy hand on my arm and steered me up the garden path. He towered over me. Even if I did run for it, I imagined him following me home, appearing like a bogeyman at the back door of my house, determined to get me. I felt I had absolutely no choice but to meekly follow him in.

'You'll get another fifty pee,' he said, as we entered the parlour. I was ink sinking into blotting paper; I disappeared with every step. And Aidan was going to blot me out, for ever.

The events that followed were painfully familiar, except that, this time, Aidan took his time. Perhaps he knew his parents were not coming back any time soon to interrupt him; perhaps he just felt more confident, second time round. But he seemed to be savouring every moment.

Aside from that, it was almost a verbatim repeat performance of the first time. The same ugly threats were issued afterwards, and again I was pushed unceremoniously out once the deed was done, this time through the door, with my fifty pence in hand. Just like the last time, I bypassed my house, unable to face it, and headed straight to the local shop to buy my pack of ten No. 6. I vainly hoped to try and rid myself of the terrible feelings that were stalking me – feelings of shock, degradation and fear – by retreating to my usual spot, at the end of the garden, and smoking my cigarettes.

Only when I felt numbed and heady did I pluck up the courage to go into the house. Once again, I faced the stark realisation that there was no one in whom I could confide, and this time I made no effort to try and explain what had become an almost intolerable secret shame.

From the time of this second incident, I felt the weight of my terrible secret even more heavily and was on constant red alert for Aidan. For him, this second incident obviously represented something of a breakthrough moment; from that point on, his attacks started to happen with chilling regularity. And, with each one, things went a bit further. It was as if he felt he owned me. As he hunted me down, the sky closed in on me. The houses and streets surrounding me became prisons. I shook uncontrollably every time I saw a red car in the distance. I went to great lengths to throw him off the scent, leaving school in the throng of the other children in the hope he wouldn't spot me. When that didn't work, I hung on until all the others had gone. I prayed that he would think he'd missed me and drive away. But it was fruitless. He was always there, waiting round the corner when I least expected it, sitting in his red Escort, engine running – a Preying Mantis.

Sometimes, he was more open in his approach and would wait for me outside the school gates. On spotting his car, I'd try and make good my escape via some other exit. I used every alternative route and shortcut I could find to try and break free from his clutches. We were playing a twisted game of cat and mouse but, unlike the cartoons that I'd always enjoyed watching, it seemed impossible to outwit my tormentor.

For more than two years, I endured this dreadful, sickening abuse. Sometimes he allowed a gap of weeks to elapse before he returned. For that brief period of freedom, I'd live with the hope that he'd stopped pursuing me. But, just when I began to relax again, he inevitably reappeared. At other times, his attacks were unremitting, coming day after day, as if he couldn't get enough of me.

Outwardly, life went on as normal. I attended school and mass and continued serving as an altar boy. Urged by my mother, who wouldn't listen to any excuse to miss mass or the sacraments, I went through the motions. I tried to be 'good', to follow the teachings of the Church and the belief that prayer was the answer to all problems. God could see a sparrow falling. His eyes were everywhere. He watched over every deed we did and suffered for our sins. But I was not aware of his suffering on the cross or his all-seeing eyes. The only eyes I feared belonged to my abuser, and he seemed to be everywhere. Not that I ever used the word 'abuser'. It had not become part of the national vocabulary and certainly was not a term I'd ever heard. The underbelly of Ireland was still hidden, and would remain hidden for a long time to come. What I was experiencing had no name and, to all outward appearances, simply did not take place.

I'd look at faces and wonder if other people possibly hid shameful secrets behind their blank expressions. I was able to do it. The only way of finding out the truth was to see inside their heads. Then I'd know if what was happening to me was also the norm for others. But I suspected that what I was enduring was unique to me. I was different to the other children. Somehow, I deserved what I was getting. I just didn't understand why.

Humiliation, fear and degradation became the fabric of my daily life, along with the bitter compensation of a fifty pence payment. My guilt became more intense as I came to rely on this money. It gave me the means to buy cigarettes. I was learning, even at this tender age, that using addictive substances was one method of steadying shredded nerves. Perhaps, the money also offered me some small sense of worth, however twisted, for my involuntary participation in this abusive relationship. At other times, I was so full of disgust that I threw the money away, not even wanting to touch it. Then I'd run home and shove the chair up against the bedroom door handle and cry into my pillow until I was exhausted and there were no tears left.

In the outside world, the effects of keeping it all to myself were starting to play out. By nature, although I was inwardly anxious, I was an outgoing and friendly child. I became increasingly shut down, jumpy and anti-social. The same harsh regime continued at home, and I didn't fare much better in school. I was disruptive in class – probably the only place where I could let off steam – often playing the clown or class rogue to the gallery of classmates, or, worse, chucking a blackboard rubber at a teacher. Punishment was the usual response to my antics, and I was on the receiving end of severe lashings.

Shut off by my secret from many of my old friends on the street, I gradually fell in with a tough crowd. Playground battles gave me an excuse to release some of my anger. Obviously, looking back from an adult perspective, my behaviour was a cry for help, for someone to stop and find out why I was so aggressive, so provocative, so challenging. Perhaps, if this had occurred, the whole sorry state of affairs would have had a chance of being exposed. But if anyone noticed, or suspected, they didn't ask, and if I had told anyone, what then? I had good reason to doubt they would believe a word I said.

At night, I would lie awake and try to figure out what was happening to me. My thoughts were reduced to their familiar chaotic tangle as I attempted to unravel the mess I was in. In the aftermath of an episode of abuse, the sequence of events always left a dream-like impression on my mind. As I sat at the table eating my dinner, walked to the shops or school, served mass, dodged a clip about the ear, it seemed impossible that, only a short while before, I'd been subjected to such vile things. But, however much I wished I was dreaming, I knew that this way of living was becoming my life.

Normality was being twisted and turned into something over which I had no control. I couldn't equate the life I was now leading with the innocent kiss I had shared with Mary. I still held on to the memory of our lips pressed together, the warm intimate feeling of being with someone who liked me as much as I liked her. I seemed to belong to two different worlds and was powerless to live in the one I wanted to live in. I knew I was losing any sense of myself. But how could I find a way out of the darkness that kept closing in on me?

The road home from school for me was like walking through a minefield, lined with opportunities for Aidan to lie in wait. During this period of abuse, I would say I was coerced over a hundred times into getting into his car or led reluctantly up his garden path.

Sadly, my experiences with Aidan marked the beginning of a domino-like sequence of abusive events that would mar my young life. And, similar to Aidan, the next one would also blind-side me, coming out of the blue.

9

Caught Off Guard

Many different types lived in our neighbourhood, including members of the Garda Síochána. They were figures of authority, and the local lads always kept well out of their way. Kicking football on the road was forbidden, so we always made sure there were no guards about when we played our matches. Some of the guards were grumpy and strict, quick to tell us off if they saw us loitering about the place, convinced, no doubt with good reason, that our minds were never far from mischief. Others were pleasant individuals who understood when to turn a blind eye on innocent pranks or a game of football. As a group, they were recognised as pillars of the community. Like priests and teachers, we were expected to look up to them as figures of authority and to give them due respect.

We were city kids and many of us had ambivalent feelings towards the gardaí. There was an accepted code of conduct between us. We would never snitch on each other to the police or make friends with a guard. Yet, we felt safe knowing they were stationed in our community. Indeed, in secret, I often fantasised about what it would be like to have a guard for my father – a law-abiding policeman who would be my own private protector.

Coming home from school was becoming even more difficult than usual. A gang of bullies often lay in wait for the kids in our neighbourhood and threw stones at us. I was becoming expert at ducking and dodging one thing or another. On one particular afternoon, I took the bus home from school and got off at a different stop than usual, to avoid the stone-throwing. In doing so, I passed a house where one of the local guards lived.

Garda McEvoy (as I've called him for the purposes of this story) was an imposing figure in his uniform. He was always smartly turned out and treated by the locals with deference. Wiry and fit, he was an active man, who created a strong presence every time he appeared in our neighbourhood. His house was impeccable, the hedge always clipped, his front garden weeded, his paintwork fresh and clean. His wife was a kindly woman with a good reputation. She dressed smartly and did the same with her children.

He was working in his garden on the other side of the

road when I hopped off the bus. When he noticed me, he waved. 'Hello there . . . could you come here for a moment?'

Though I recognised him, I had never actually spoken to Garda McEvoy before. I crossed the road to his wooden gate. His garden was neat with a trimmed privet hedge and rows of pink and yellow border plants. He was a tall man and, as I looked up at him, I can remember thinking he had smooth skin for a tough cop, very clean-shaven. He was off duty, wearing casual but clean-cut clothes. He was friendly and chatty, asking me if I'd been to school and what I thought about my teachers. It was a typical adult-to-child conversation, the topics safe and familiar.

I responded chattily to his questions, pleased that someone of his stature was taking the time to talk to me. After a few minutes, Garda McEvoy paused in thought, then said, 'Listen, would you give me a hand to move something?'

I agreed without question and followed him up the garden path and in through the open front door. I laid down my satchel on the doormat. He gestured towards the back and, when I went ahead of him, I heard the front door click behind me. Of course, I should have been suspicious. I'd heard too many locks click and seal off my escape, but I was only conscious of a sense of self-importance. I was being asked to help someone whose job involved helping others. The gardens were fairly big in his road, so I figured I would be asked to cut the grass or help him fell a tree.

We got to the kitchen, which was straight down the corridor from the front door. I hesitated, not sure if I should approach the back door, and he gestured again that I go ahead of him. I was halfway across the kitchen when he suddenly came close to me and spun me around. I was stopped in my tracks but, before I could react, he slipped his right hand down my trousers. As he groped me, he pressed my face into his rock-hard chest. I was completely stunned at the suddenness of his attack.

The same pattern, the same shock, the same shamed outrage. Yet, this was different again. Here was a figure of authority. A word from him, a nod, an accusation could put me in jail. Who would stop him? I couldn't think of a single person who would stand up to him. I understood what was going to happen. I knew how I was going to feel afterwards. I also knew I would never dare to speak to anyone about it.

It seemed as if I watched from a great distance as he opened his own fly and went through the same familiar routine. It was over quickly, and he zipped himself up, whisked me around and frogmarched me down the hall. He unlocked the door and pushed me out. He had not spoken a single word to me throughout the whole ordeal. Within a few minutes of our initial conversation at the front gate, I was outside again, clutching my satchel to my chest. The door snapped shut behind me.

As I stumbled down the road, I would have looked like any ordinary nine-year-old-boy, satchel over my shoulder, shoes scuffed. People passed by but no one glanced in my direction. There should be some sign, something to signify what had just occurred in this respectable, well-furnished house with its tidy front garden. As I neared home, my horror increased at the thought that Garda McEvoy might be in touch with my mother, accusing me of some wrong-doing. To me, he represented an even more frightening threat than Aidan, whom I despised but who did not have the power to imprison me. I wandered past the house, then became instantly worried in case Aidan was lurking somewhere. I turned and darted around to the back of the house and in through the kitchen door, which thankfully was open.

I dumped my satchel and rushed upstairs to get my secret stash of cigarettes. In my hideaway at the bottom of the garden, I lit up and smoked three in a row. Somehow, I had to make sense of these episodes. Perhaps this was the normal thing for grown-ups to do to children. Admittedly, no one ever spoke about it, but lots of things, like how babies got into mothers' tummies or not having enough money to pay bills, were never discussed yet they happened all the time.

If my father was alive I could confide in him. His absence from my life had turned him into a mythical figure who knew the answer to everything and the solution to all of life's problems. I could ask one of my uncles if this was normal behaviour. If I mentioned it to the lads after we'd played a game of football, they might tell me that they also had similar things done to them. Then I'd no longer feel so different. But even as these thoughts crossed my mind, I dismissed them. Nothing normal was going on in my life. I thought of Mr Conroy, his kindness and his easy way of talking. I always felt safe with him – and that was how it should be with adults. Children were supposed to be safe in their company. If they were not, then who was to blame? For all my musings, I was no wiser and no nearer to understanding how Garda McEvoy, our brave guardian of the law, had turned out to be such a disgusting phoney.

I vowed that I would never get off the bus near his house again. Nor would I ever give any grown-up a 'hand', no matter how nicely they asked. I would rather run the risk of having stones lobbed at me by the local yobs than endure another sordid encounter with this 'respectable' pillar of our community.

A few days later, Garda McEvoy passed our house on his way to mass, accompanied by his wife and children. As usual, they were all smartly dressed. He was in a shirt, tie, black suit and his long black overcoat. From my front window, I noticed everything about him, his confident strut, his polished shoes, his proud stance that seemed to command deference. I looked at his children's faces. But I knew I would not see anything other than the normal expression of children on their way to mass and communion. He was a model citizen, father, husband, proudly holding his unsuspecting wife on his arm. She had probably mopped the kitchen floor. The thought made my stomach turn, as did the sight of him.

I longed to run to the door and shout something obscene at him. I fantasised about rushing up to his wife and saying, 'Do you know what your God-fearing husband did to me in your kitchen two days ago?' But, of course, I did nothing. My anger was volcanic but futile. The world no longer made sense. Who could I turn to? Who was actually trustworthy?

He didn't even glance in the direction of our house as he passed by and continued his journey towards the church. I wondered if he would ask God for forgiveness? And, if he did, would he be forgiven? Maybe by God, but certainly not by me.

10

The Ultimate Violation

Aidan raped me for the first time around a month after the Garda McEvoy incident. The memory of that day will remain forever imprinted on my mind. It was an unusual day in the Devane household, as perparations were underway for a knees up. One of my sisters was doing a steady line, and she brought her boyfriend home to meet the family. A party of any sort was a rare event in our house. It lightened my mother's mood and it was nice to have more people around as they prepared for the guests to arrive. I was excited and didn't mind having to give up my bed and sleep on cushions on the floor.

Before the gathering got underway, I was out playing with some of the lads in 'The Wire', a piece of ground where we often gathered. I was walking home when I realised Aidan's car was trailing me. He kerb-crawled for a few minutes, then parked his car further ahead on my side of the road. When I passed by, my head bent down, studiously ignoring him, he drove on again. He remained one jump ahead of me and parked the car on the kerbside again, trying to cut me off. The earlier excitement was knocked out of me, and I was overwhelmed once again by the daily gloom and dread. I envisaged Aidan's tatty trousers, his dark greasy hair, his dirty fingernails, his unshaven face, his black teeth, and felt as if the Grim Reaper had come for me too soon. Death and Aidan were becoming synonymous in my mind and I believed I'd never be strong enough to fight him off.

That Saturday afternoon ended in the same grimy situation as it always did, in his front parlour. His touch still made me want to vomit, but I had become adept at blocking out what was happening, detaching and floating out, over my body. During these times, I was a stranger to myself, watching from a distance. From my 'floating' position, I would focus on other things, banal things – the floral wallpaper or the dirty white Venetian blinds – anything that wasn't Aidan and what was happening to me. Sometimes I would just count in my head. In some small way, this helped to blot out the unspeakable sensations that I had to endure. If I looked at him, I was lost.

The hardest part was when he squashed me into the rough carpet, his full weight upon me. I feared that I was going to suffocate or have an asthma attack. The carpet always burned my cheeks but I knew now that the end was near. Another few minutes and I'd be free, the fifty-pence piece hot in my hand. Suddenly, I heard a key turn in the front door.

Aidan froze and then, quick as a flash, rolled off me and zipped up his fly. As I pulled up my shorts, he rushed to the window and lifted the blinds. Light slanted into the room, and the shabby décor stood out in sharp relief. How I hated this place, this prison from which there was no escape. Aidan looked angry and desperate at the same time. In that same instant, knowing that someone else had entered the house and could possibly enter the room, I shared his fear of discovery. Somehow, without knowing how, I, the victim, had become complicit in the rituals of my aggressor.

He didn't hesitate. For the second time since our initial meeting, I was pushed unceremoniously out the window. I landed on the dirt below and stood up. Now that I was free and undiscovered, I wanted to weep with relief at the unseen person's untimely return to the house.

Aidan hung his sweaty face out the window. His eyes glistened. He was obviously still in a fever of lust. 'I'll see you at the top of the road – ten minutes.' He must have seen my jaw drop because he leaned further out and put his face close to mine. 'You'll be there, or you'll be dead,' he whispered hoarsely. 'Understand?'

I understood. There was no escape. I scrambled to my feet and ran down the path, then out onto the road. My face burned from the rough carpet but that was nothing compared to the fear in my chest. I ran until I reached my house. The door was closed. For once, there were more people inside than just my mother and siblings.

I hesitated. Aidan had said ten minutes, and five had passed. What should I do? My mother hadn't believed me the first time I tried to explain but that was over two years ago. Would it be possible for me to say something again? I had discovered a word for Aidan. 'Pervert' was what the older boys called people like him. Their school-yard slang had given me a vague understanding of this furtive underworld, but I wondered how many of them had an image in their mind of what a pervert looked like. If they had never experienced the touch of one, they probably imagined them as cartoon villains. But I saw those perverts at mass. I watched them bow their heads and receive communion. I saw them upholding the law.

Terrified, I stood outside my house, convinced my life was in danger. Aidan had finally decided to make good his threats to kill me, afraid I was going to reveal our terrible secret. Eventually, I made my decision. I would tell someone, anyone who answered the door. Laughter floated from the front room. The door was opened by a man I knew. He was obviously having a good old time at the celebration. He looked flushed, and there was a strong smell of drink from him.

I sensed a car passing behind me and turned to see Aidan in his red Escort. He drove to the top of the road and parked on our side of the triangle. Panicked, I felt pressure in my bladder and had an urgent need to pee. Tears pricked my eyes. I desperately needed the help of someone who could put an end to his reign of terror.

'What are you waiting for? Come on in, John.' The man gestured at me to come inside and join the fun.

I didn't know what to say, or how to start, but I believed he would intervene and end my suffering. I took a deep breath and blurted out the first words I could think of. 'There's a man, yer man there' – I pointed to the red Escort parked by the church. Aidan was now out of the car, standing beside it, looking straight at us. It was a surreal moment, like a stand-off in the westerns I'd seen on TV.

'That man standing at the car is doing things to me, horrible things, and he wants me to go with him . . .' My voice trailed away.

My companion looked up the road in the direction I was pointing. I thought, just for a moment, that he was going to dash up the road and attack Aidan. I wanted to be the one to do it, to kill him with my bare hands, but I needed an adult's strength to see him off finally and forever. But this man to whom I had entrusted my secret simply stepped backwards into the house and said over my shoulder, 'Sure by the time I get up there, he'll be gone.' With that parting comment, he closed the door.

I couldn't believe it. I pushed the door with my hands and it wouldn't budge. Feeling defeated, I knelt down on the step and started to cry. I was looking into a black chasm. His indifference confirmed my suspicions that adults knew but didn't care that people like Aidan existed. They expected me to do what I was told, even if every part of my being hated doing it.

That instant of abandonment was a turning point in my young life. Adults were not prepared to help. My mother had made this perfectly clear. Now this man had confirmed it. And Aidan, still standing by his car and smoking a cigarette, was waiting for me.

When he realised I was alone again, he beckoned to me. I could read his body language and knew he was becoming irritated. He was silently signalling that I had better get into his car this instant or he would kill me.

I knelt on the step for a second longer, but I knew I had no option, nowhere else to turn. I left the noise of the house behind. In a trance-like state, I walked down the path towards Aidan. As I reached the car, he leaned over and opened the door on my side. It was business as usual. Once seated, he leaned across and locked my door.

He drove away from the estate. This was a new experience. We'd never gone anywhere except to his place before now. Now I genuinely believed I was going to my death. I had been threatened so often that I believed it was only a matter of time. I'd heard horror stories on the news about people like Ian Brady and knew that grown-ups could kill kids. I'd seen Myra Hindley's hard eyes staring out at me from photographs. They buried children on the moors and their bodies were never found. My terror increased as Aidan drove deeper into the countryside. As the journey continued, I felt my fear turn to resignation. He could do what he liked with me, I didn't care any more. If I was going to be killed and buried, there was no point in trying to fight it.

I eventually recognised a familiar landmark. We were in a place called Ballyclough, near Limerick Golf Club and an army firing range. There were few houses on the road. The lanes were so narrow and winding that he would have had to reverse if he met another car. But there was no traffic passing by that night.

Eventually, he stopped the car. We were in an isolated place, near a gate which opened onto a firing range. We had gone a few yards up a dirt track. Tall hedges bordered the car on either side. This was no random location. It had been chosen in the knowledge that no one would spot his car. We sat in silence for a brief period. Numbed, not knowing what would happen next, I waited. Suddenly, he started turning the knob on the side of my seat. I was thrown backwards and found myself staring at a grey car ceiling. He turned the knob on his own seat, so both our seats were reclined together. I held my breath as he climbed on top of me. I noticed a tear in the ceiling above my seat and focused on it. His weight pressed against me, and I thought in that instant that he was going to choke me. I stared harder at the tear on the filthy ceiling and willed myself to disappear through it.

He levered himself up to his knees and forced me onto my front, just as always. My head was crushed up against the headrest. This time, however, he pulled my shorts down past my knees, removing one leg from one side of them. I was struggling to catch my breath. Suddenly, excruciating pain ripped through my body. I realised that he was pushing his penis inside me.

I screamed. Instead of the torn ceiling, I had an image of the crucifixion. This must be how Jesus felt as he was nailed to the cross. As Aidan raped me, I fought the urge to be sick. In my short lifetime, I'd been punched and kicked. I'd been beaten endlessly with wooden spoons, canes, whatever came to hand, but what was happening to me now, in this isolated place, was beyond anything I had ever experienced. Darkness filled the car. There was nothing except pain and noise as Aidan brutalised me. He shouted filthy obscenities at me, as if in a rage. I pleaded with God to make it stop. My head was crushed against the headrest, and I thought I would pass out. I could not, now, describe the details of what Aidan did to me that time in his car. It is too brutal, too crude, too painful to remember. But, when it was finally over, I wished that I was dead.

He then turned the key in the ignition and started doing a three-point turn. It would not have surprised me if we had been driving to my death. I had no idea what he was going to do next. I recited prayers that I'd learned as an altar boy in my mind and stared bleakly into the dark.

Aidan did not utter a word as the pitch-black country darkness gave way to the yellow city lights. We were heading back home. I was still in a complete daze, staring out at the rows of bleak houses as they flashed past. We finally reached the statue of Our Lady Queen of Peace. Aidan leaned over and opened the lock on my door, indicating that I should get out.

I hesitated. Not even fifty pence this time? To ask for it meant having to speak to him, and I'd had nothing to say to this brute. I would probably have flung the money away but it seemed so wrong that what he had done to me should be entirely free.

It's easy with hindsight to look back and try to understand the confusion that raged inside me. I hated the money this vile person gave me yet, in my demented state, this exchange was part of our unspeakable transaction. It was no compensation for what he was doing to me, but to leave me without it stripped away one more layer of my humanity. Without the money, I was his slave. I was his slave regardless of how much he paid me, but this devalued my suffering even more. Another part of me believed I had sold my soul to the Devil and he would keep coming back for more.

Aidan drove away, after uttering the usual dire threats. I was aware that it was now very late and I risked being punished. I shuffled awkwardly, taking small steps, so obliterated by the experience that I could barely focus on walking up the garden path. My bottom hurt unmercifully and there seemed to be liquid seeping into my pants. I was terrified it would flow down my legs, and there would be no way of hiding it.

I stood on the doorstep, shuddering. Bernard answered the door. I pushed past him and mounted the stairs. Alone at last, I sat on the bed and gingerly let my buttocks relax for the first time. I took my shorts and pants down and examined their contents. To my horror, there was blood in the thick fluid. Still shaking, I put on my dressing gown and got some toilet paper to dry myself off. The bleeding continued and I was scared. I felt like a rag doll whose insides were coming apart.

I returned to my room, lay on my bed and began to shake uncontrollably. I replayed the scene over and over in my mind. The man on the doorstep, my plea for help. How could he close the door on me? This betrayal burned inside me. I wiped my eyes on my sleeve and wondered how I would hide the mess. How would I explain it if my mother saw my pants? I took them off, rolled them in a ball and hid them. I touched my bum with my fingers and winced: it was a raw, open wound. The next day, I would scrub my pants in secret, in a desperate bid to rub out all signs of Aidan's violation. But that night it was all I could do to crawl under my sheets and lie down in the foetal position, listening to the laughter and voices downstairs. I wasn't even able to cry. What good were tears? I could cry a river and it would make no difference. I wished that Aidan had actually killed me with his bare hands. I felt half-dead already and, that night, I would have welcomed death with open arms.

11

The Paedophile Ring

After the violent rape by Aidan, I remained in shock for days. My body was wracked with pain. But, rather than outrage, which I felt keenly, my overriding emotion was one of guilt. One of the most devastating effects of sexual abuse and 'grooming' is that children become convinced they have brought it on themselves. I'd battled with such feelings ever since my first encounter with Aidan, and each subsequent episode only served to reinforce them. On some level, I was in the wrong. I got what I deserved.

Strangely, Aidan disappeared for a while after this episode. Perhaps he feared he had gone too far this time and was lying low until the dust settled and I was once again lulled into a false sense of security. I can only speculate, and it didn't matter anyway. His physical disappearance did nothing to alleviate his presence. My nostrils were filled with his stench. I can still feel his presence, even as I write these lines. Every time I closed my eyes, I was back in the car, my face pressed up hard against the headrest, my body being brutally violated. Unable to keep my eyes shut, I'd lie awake and still imagine his features contorted with lust. I hid under the sheets, terrified he might actually come and get me again. And the hardest part of all was the feeling that I had nowhere to turn.

For days after the rape, blood streaks appeared on the toilet paper when I wiped myself. The blood scared me. I was terrified he had done something to me that couldn't be mended. How could I explain such injuries to a doctor? I carefully felt myself with my fingertips. Although I seemed to be back to normal on the outside, I dreaded finding out what might have been done to my insides. Even on the sunniest of days, that fear never lifted. Indeed, the memory of that rape haunts me to this day.

Aidan had left a permanent reminder inside me and I still felt discomfort when I was walking. But, after a couple of weeks had passed and I hadn't seen him on the street, I began to believe he had finally lost interest in me. I wasn't yet able to relax fully, but I thought that maybe what had happened that last time might have satisfied his perverted appetite, and he no longer needed me.

If it was over, I was hugely relieved yet, strangely, a small part of me missed not having attention from someone. With every fibre of my being, I hated what had happened with him, so this conflicting emotion of feeling lonely for the attention I received from him compounded my sense of shame and self-disgust. How could I be a normal boy if I could miss that kind of attention?

I had been 'groomed' from the age of eight to behave in a sexual way towards a grown-up man but, back then, I had no way of understanding the complexities of grooming. Again, with the wisdom of hindsight, I understand what I was experiencing. I was starved of attention and proper care. My home life was in chaos, my mother always preoccupied. I was an outsider at school with no real friends. Feeling small and overpowered had become the norm for me, and my sordid experiences with Aidan, no matter how revolting, meant that I was noticed. This lack of care from the adult world was why I'd been so vulnerable to his attentions, and why I kept on complying with his wishes, despite how I felt about them.

My relief at Aidan's disappearance was to be short-lived. As it transpired, while lying low, he was also organising his next move in the grooming process. After a few weeks of not seeing him, I began to relax, no longer on my guard the way I had been before. Then, one day, as I left school and turned the corner, there he was, hovering at the kerb-side, in his dreaded red Escort. My heart stopped. My instinct was to run. But, as usual, I stood rooted to the spot. The engine was running. He started driving slowly towards me.

The hold Aidan had over me was forged out of sheer psychological terror. Now it had become overlaid with the threat of rape. This act had represented the final conquering.

Aidan, I believe, now felt as if he actually owned me. He leaned out of the window, looking almost kindly at me. 'Come on, I'll give you a lift home.'

I felt nailed to the pavement – fearful of saying anything at all, of moving, of breathing, of getting in the car, or of not getting in the car. My hesitation always riled him, and he soon adopted a familiar hectoring tone to intimidate me into obedience: 'Get in the fuckin' car, or I'll be telling your mammy what you're up to, and, so help me, I'll kill you both.'

That was it. This threat to my mother and to me was more frightening than the threat of his physical molestation. Once again, I was caught between a rock and a hard place. I swallowed and got in the car, holding my satchel between my legs as I always did in an attempt to defend myself. Aidan leaned over and pushed down the lock on my door. The smell of his fetid armpits and dog breath was as rotten as ever. Nothing had changed. We drove on in silence.

I watched the houses and people flashing by. If only they knew what was happening to me in this clapped-out car. The past couple of weeks, without his constant pestering, had allowed me to breathe normally again. But I should have known he'd be back, just as soon as his lust got the better of him. I just hoped against hope that it wouldn't be a repetition of our last encounter. I squeezed my thighs together tightly, feeling sick at the thought of what was to follow.

We were driving to an entirely new part of town. I was unable to recognise any familiar landmarks. I glanced sideways at Aidan. His unshaven jaw was set, and lank hair framed his grimy face, just as always. His expression gave away nothing.

We finally drew up outside a very dilapidated house on what I later knew was the Dublin Road, across the road from St Patrick's School. Aidan got out the car and proceeded around to my side to unlock my door. I followed like a prisoner heading for jail. Without a word, Aidan indicated I should go up the path. The gate was hanging off the posts, the garden overgrown, the path weedy and broken. The house resembled something out of a horror movie. I turned to run, but he was behind me. Before I could make good my escape, he grabbed me and turned me back. I stumbled forward.

He held firmly on to my arm, his grip dug into my flesh, as he knocked on the door with his free hand. Later, I would see the bruises. The door opened a crack and a horrible stench wafted out of the house. A grizzled grey head appeared, an old man with a wrinkled face and tombstone teeth. Without a word, the old man opened the door and let Aidan and me in.

The hall was in total disarray, covered with cardboard boxes, books, food cans and newspapers, all overlaid with a thick layer of dust and grime. It was clear he and Aidan knew each other, and the old man indicated we go upstairs, which we did, single file. At the back of the rambling house, along a dingy, cluttered landing, was a room with its windows blacked out. The same dreaded fear of being murdered crept over me.

The room was filled with photographic equipment: big silver lights, white screens, rolls of film, cameras and sheets of coloured cellophane hanging from the ceiling. I was shown to a stool and Aidan pushed me down onto it. 'Stay there, if you know what's good for you,' he barked.

Then he and the man went into the corner of the room and whispered together. I glanced around at the open door and again made a run for it. But Aidan was too quick for me.

'Where d'you think you're going?' He blocked my exit and caught me by the throat. I was flung back onto the stool with so much force that it, and I, fell over. 'This is Sean, he wants to photograph you.'

I scrambled back to my feet as Sean shuffled over and looked me up and down. His shabby old trousers were held up by braces. 'Ever had your photo taken?' He had bleary blue eyes and wispy hair and must have been seventy at least.

I nodded meekly. I'd had school photos done. But that was no comparison to what was going on here. Aidan stood with his back against the door, watching as Sean started his 'session' with me. Was this part of Aidan's plot to kill me? What had he told Sean? I thought of the last night in the car and was terrified they were both going to do the same thing to me. I had never been so scared in my life.

How could I, even for a crazy instant, have missed the attention I received from this filthy man? He had a vice-like hold over me and now I was in an even worse situation than ever. I was only ten and I was going to die.

'Stand up.' Sean sounded gruff. I obeyed his order. He indicated with a gnarled finger that I should go and stand in front of a big white screen hanging from the ceiling. He flicked on the large lights and I was suddenly blinded. I couldn't see either him, behind his camera on a tripod, or Aidan, behind him, over by the door.

'Take your jacket off, and your shirt,' he said.

'Wha . . .?' I found my voice, finally.

'Just do it.'

Horrified, I did as I was told. Sean started snapping. 'You're very photogenic, did you know that?' he said.

'Photogen . . .?'

'You look good in the pictures,' he said, 'you've a fine face.' He was obviously trying to coax me on. He snapped away for a minute or two. Is this it? I thought. Is this all he wants? I began to relax a small bit. Perhaps it would be OK after all.

Suddenly, Sean appeared beside me. I recoiled from his awful body odour. He bent down, knees cracking, and put his bleary face into mine. I got a whiff of alcohol. 'Like to earn a pound?' he said.

A pound? Had Aidan told him what I had done for fifty pence? I sought out Aidan, but he was no longer there.

'Where's Aidan?'

'Don't worry, he'll be back soon enough.' Sean almost sounded nice for a moment. 'Like to earn a pound?' he repeated, doggedly.

'Doing what?'

'Pull your bottoms down and let me take a photo of you.'

I gasped. The thought of taking off my clothes in front of this dirty old man disgusted me. He must have read my mind.

'Listen,' he brought his ugly face close to mine again, 'it'll be over in a trice. Just a couple of shots, then a pound in your hand. OK?'

I thought about it. I could get a pound and then it would be over.

'That's all?' I was suspicious.

'That's all, promise.'

I looked at him, feeling disgusted, but knew from bitter experience that my only option was to just get it over with and get out of this filthy hovel.

The man disappeared over to the side of the room and returned with something sloshing around in a dirty glass. 'Drink this.'

'What is it?'

'Just drink it.'

I took the glass and looked its contents. I smelled it, afraid it was poison. It had the unmistakable odour of booze. I sipped it. It was strong, brown and syrupy. I drank it down, and it spread a warm glow down my throat and into my tummy. Sean came and took the glass.

'Better?'

I didn't say anything, but I did feel slightly woozy, a frothy feeling in my head.

'OK, slip down your pants.'

I did as bid. I had sold my soul to the devil and now I was keeping company with his older brother. Sean began snapping away. My head felt really buzzy now, and I couldn't see him for the blinding lights he had on to take the photos.

He then spread out a dirty old sheepskin rug and instructed me to lie on top of it. He came over and poured more booze in my glass from a brown bottle – I think it was some brand of sherry – and made me knock it back. Then he snapped away furiously, instructing me to take up various provocative poses. I felt ashamed but I did what he told me.

The lights then dimmed, and he came over and proceeded to do precisely what I dreaded might happen. But by now I was too drunk to do anything about it. After he forced me to conduct oral sex, I began to wretch. Sean, who was now cleaning himself up on a green towel, didn't glance in my direction. 'Be sick in this,' he snapped. He handed me a filthy silver spittoon. I vomited into it. Then I started crying.

'Put your clothes on – here's your pound,' he barked.

I got myself dressed as fast as I could, snatched the pound, then rushed over to the door, desperate to escape. But Sean was no longer interested in me and offered no resistance. He unlocked the door and shoved me out onto the landing. Aidan was waiting at the bottom of the stairs. He opened the front door and I followed him out, tears rolling down my face. We got in his car in silence. I had no idea if he was going to do the same thing again to me.

Thankfully, however, he dropped me off, as always at the Statue of Our Lady Queen of Peace at the top of our road. Without a word, I got out of the car, slammed the door, and staggered home, full of disgust. Once again, the boundaries had been shifted, pushed beyond what I could have imagined possible. Was there no end to this horror? Upstairs and alone, I washed my mouth out with carbolic soap, over and over, trying to eradicate the traces of what had happened.

Even now, I vividly remember the horror of that day. 'Abuse' has a smell. It is foul and, once you've picked up on it, it stays with you. Abuse hurts, terrifies, shames and destroys. It creates memories that can never be eradicated. These encounters are etched into my brain. My soul is seared. When I read back what I've written, my stomach churns, and I'm a small boy again, struggling with demons, supping with evil.

But what I write gives a shape, however harsh, to those brutal encounters. These days, words like 'abuse', 'paedophile', 'oral sex', 'porn industry', 'victim' are commonplace. They resonate with meaning. In recent decades, Ireland's seedy underbelly has been well and truly slit open. There terms are some of its entrails, and the word 'paedophilia' has become almost sanitised through our collective indignation, as evidenced in the endless reportage in the media and outraged calls to programmes such as *Liveline*.

When I decided to write my story, I wanted to describe the real-life experience that lay behind such words. And I feel driven to bear witness to the suffering of countless anonymous young people, who in the past were terrified to stand up for themselves. Who were afraid to run forward in case they ran towards death. Who were afraid to speak up because they had no language. Who, even if they did succeed in finding the courage to tell the truth, would discover that the so-called caring adults, the pillars of our community, recoiled in disgust. Some would have recoiled in genuine denial, others in anger and outrage at such 'imaginings'. Others, knowing the truth, would have turned their backs because a child's cry is easily drowned out.

12

Visitors from Dublin

Sean was the first of a series of paedophiles from around the Limerick area to whom Aidan introduced me in the months to come. I was taken back to the old man's house for photographic sessions on a number of occasions. To my amazement, I sometimes met other boys there. There must have been at least five others like myself, none of whom I recognised. At last, I had an answer to one of my questions. I was not unique in my situation. The same things happened to other boys. We largely ignored each other, silenced and intimidated by what was happening to us, no doubt each feeling his own personal shame. Plied with drink, we were forced to strip off and pose provocatively. We were forced to masturbate for the photographer, sometimes together, or to pleasure the other men who often turned up there to watch.

At one of these sessions, I recognised one of the men in

attendance. He was a bald, plump, middle-aged man, whom I knew to be married. He was also a garda – though not Garda McEvoy.

On other occasions, Aidan drove me to a different garda's house in a part of Limerick I didn't recognise. This garda would get out a big stick to 'discipline' me, which he would bring down heavily and repeatedly on my naked behind. When my skin was red and sore, he would rub it in a bid 'to make the pain go away', while masturbating himself. Nothing surprised me any more. It was just another form of degradation that I had to endure. Afterwards, I would be given a pound and dropped at Our Lady's statue, with the usual threats from Aidan to keep quiet.

I lived constantly with a sickening feeling of dread in my stomach. Nothing could banish it. I no longer believed there was any escape, and no one, not even God, was listening. I wanted to die but I didn't know how to go about ending my life.

In hindsight, I know that Aidan was part of a paedophile ring, although back then we simply called them 'pervs'. I now believe that the photographs would have been shown around the ring, so that each man could pick the child he wanted to abuse. Sean and Aidan appeared to be the 'leaders', with Aidan ferrying the kids to different destinations. Our flesh was cheap. These men could have sex with us for as little as fifty pence or a pound.

Our souls were in danger. While the priests preached about chastity and referred to our bodies as 'temples of the

Holy 'Spirit', these men helped themselves to our flesh. We heard about the Lamb of God and went like lambs to the slaughter, the threat of death constantly hanging over us. These men operated with impunity. They played on the guilt, made us terrified of exposure, convinced us we were responsible for what was being done to us.

At night, I would bury my face in the pillow in a desperate bid to blot out as much as I could. Meanwhile, Aidan would continue to 'come and get me' just for himself when I was on my way home from school. I never knew what was going to happen next: would I be servicing just him, or his perverted friends as well?

The deeper I became embroiled in the 'ring', the more I learned to block things out. I put the lid on a sordid Pandora's box and hoped against hope that nothing would ever push its way out. Away from home, I was trapped in my secret life, and equally trapped in my house where I lived in dread of my mother's anger and the terrifying repercussions of anyone finding out what was going on. I smoked compulsively – after all, I now had the money to buy as many Players No. 6 as I needed. Not ones and twos but packs of twenty.

Nothing stays the same. Sometimes things improve; other times, you just get deeper into trouble. Soon I would be freed from the web of abuse I was in – only to open the door to something far more destructive, which was to unfold on the rough docklands of my own proud city.

*

I was eleven years old when my mother went on another trip to Dublin, this time with a couple of her friends. By now, my sisters had flown the nest, and Bernard and myself lived alone in the house with her, apart from a succession of lodgers she took in, to help with the finances.

When Mammy departed like this, things inevitably descended into anarchy at home. Food became scarce and, just as the last time she'd disappeared to Dublin, Bernard and I ended up living on scraps from the fridge. I had smoked all my earnings away and had no money to go out and buy more food.

When she returned a few days later, she had an announcement to make. 'There's two young men coming down to stay with us for a few nights – you'll give them your room, John.'

I looked at her in astonishment, but she gave no further explanation. I made her tea, and she took her cup into the living room to watch television. Agnes saw herself as a 'Good Samaritan'– she was capable of kindness to strangers yet I could never experience the same warmth from her.

The next day, she explained that on her weekend in Dublin, she'd met two young men in a pub. They were desperate to get away from the city as soon as they could and had confided their problems to her. She was convinced they were nice young men, and she was going to help them. Until they had sorted out the trouble they were in, they would stay with us.

Two days later, the two Dubliners arrived. It was around teatime and I was out in the back garden when the doorbell rang. I ran in, but Mammy got to the door first. Looking from behind her, I saw them on our doorstep, each holding a small bag. They looked to be in their late teens or early twenties. One was clean-shaven with fair hair. He had attractive blue eyes and a pretty, almost effeminate face. The other was of chunky build with sandy-coloured hair. He was unshaven and less fashionably dressed than his companion. They were obviously pleased to be here, and my mother was friendly and animated with them. This side of Mammy was very unfamiliar to me, and I was intrigued to get a glimpse of what she must be like when she was out enjoying herself with her friends.

For the purposes of this book, the blond guy was called Danny and the darker guy was Diarmuid. 'My God, am I happy to be here!' Danny said emphatically. 'You're taking us out of a living hell, so you are.'

They came into the living room, and Mammy got out a couple of bottles of Guinness. They toasted each other and us. I was both fascinated and excited by them. They were from the capital city, their accents were different and, to me, they seemed quite sophisticated, yet friendly and full of fun. I felt my spirits lift. Perhaps life would get better with these Dubliners around; perhaps there'd be company for me, people to talk to at last.

Mammy busied herself in the kitchen, cooking them a supper of pork chops, apple sauce and potatoes, followed by red jelly and ice cream. It was a feast and she was in her element, playing the hostess. I was amazed at her transformation and felt a twinge of jealousy that they were getting all this fuss and attention.

I sat listening to Danny, the blond Dubliner, who was also the more talkative of the two. He explained that they had been working for a man who installed double-glazing. Their job had been to go round and get orders from people, who had to pay up front. They would pass on the money to their boss. There was only problem: the double-glazing never got installed. The boss kept the money and swindled the people instead. Now, a Sunday newspaper had done an investigation into this man's business, and his scam was going to be exposed the coming weekend. It was obvious that the article would lead the gardaí to the man, and then to the boys, his employees. They had decided, having met my mother in a pub last weekend and told her the whole sorry story, that this was the moment to leave. They'd done a runner, hitched a lift and now had arrived at their hiding place in Limerick: our house. Their plan was to spend some time with us, before finding digs in the city.

Over the course of fifteen years, Mammy kept lodgers, so it was not unusual for people to stay at our house. But I would soon discover this pair were far different to the other good people who shared our home.

After supper, I cleared the table while Mammy got ready for her trip to the pub. I assumed the Dublin lads would be going with her and felt a twinge of disappointment that they were leaving so soon. While I was moving back and forth from the kitchen to the living room, they joked and laughed with her. It was a revelation, hearing Agnes sounding so young and carefree. She seemed so comfortable with them, like they were old friends.

I heard Danny, the blond guy, asking her if she knew Cecil Street or Lower Cecil Street? 'We've been told there's a couple of nice pubs down there,' he said. 'Could you tell us how to get there?'

'Sure, I know it like the back of my hand,' said Mammy.

I knew this area, too. The General Post Office was there, and I usually collected my mother's benefits each week on a Saturday. Mammy was now ready to go out, handbag in hand and her coat on. They were relaxing on the sofa, looking totally at ease in their new environment, and it was obvious they were not going to accompany her. I surveyed the scene as I moved back and forth from the back room to the kitchen, clearing up after supper.

When I'd finished, I went in to say goodnight. Mammy turned to me. 'John knows the way to Cecil Street, don't you John? He'll take you down.' It wasn't a request, it was an order.

'Sure, I'll be happy to.' I was delighted not to have to go to bed at the usual time and jumped straight to it, pulling on my shoes and jacket, determined to show off my city to these sophisticated Dubliners.

The guys got up off the sofa, stretched and yawned. As

Mammy went to the front door, she turned and warned me to come straight home. I nodded, unable to hide my delight at this turn of events.

'John! Y'hear?' she repeated. 'No dawdling on the way back.'

'Don't worry, Mammy,' I assured her, 'I'll be straight home.'

With that, she disappeared into the night to meet her friends, and I headed off with the Dublin lads to direct them to a pub, which we'll call The Penthouse. Danny, in particular, was chatty. He kept asking questions as we walked down town: How old was I? Did I go to school? Was I an altar boy? What music did I like? I'd no idea where The Penthouse was, but I found it without too much difficulty. When we reached it, I prepared to turn for home. Danny invited me to stay and have a drink with them.

I shook my head, surprised that a grown-up would invite me into a pub. 'I'd like to, but I've got to get home. Mammy will be angry if I'm late.'

'Go on,' he said, persuasively. 'One won't hurt.' Danny pulled me by the arm, and Diarmuid followed us in silence. It was clear that Danny was the 'main man' and Diarmuid his sidekick. I hesitated at the door. As I looked inside, I saw it was full of men, with very few women. Through the dark, smoky atmosphere, I could make out that many of the men were flamboyantly dressed.

Danny strode straight up to the bar and ordered the

drinks, and I soon found myself with a real grown-up alcoholic drink in my hand, a scotch and red lemonade. I was eleven years old and inside a pub for the first time in my life. This was turning out to be a great night. The long wooden bar was of the old-fashioned variety, with an elderly man serving behind it. I stood at one end, with the Dubliners next to me, hiding me from view. The drink went straight to my head. I felt light-headed and, unusually for me, free of anxiety. It was a wonderful feeling. As I looked around, I saw a couple of boys in the premises, not much older than I.

Standing at the bar, Danny continued to ask me questions about myself. I'd never felt so important before and didn't want the evening to end. But I knew that being there with them was a risky business. Even if Mammy didn't witness my return, Bernard would tell on me if I was late or smelled of alcohol.

I told Danny that my mother would go mad if she knew what I was doing but he just laughed and told me about the pub where they'd met her in Dublin. Like The Penthouse, it too had a reputation for being a poets' pub, full of arty-farty people, so he'd tell my mother that having a drink here was part of my further education. We all laughed at this, even though I didn't get the joke. I was having a whale of time. As we drank, I began to notice that the lads held their glasses in a particular way, with their little fingers sticking out.

'Why are you doing that?' I pointed to their fingers. They exchanged glances, and Danny laughed.

'Oh, it's just a fashionable thing to do, holding your pinky out like a lady.' I mimicked him, holding my glass in the same way. I wanted to be like these guys – they were cool grown-ups, and I was part of their gang. For tonight, at least.

'How about another?' asked Danny.

'Go on then, why not?' I felt devilish and carefree. I noticed, as Danny got the drinks in, that Diarmuid was smoking in a funny way, too. He held his cigarette like my mother did, up in the air, level to his chin. Then, as he exhaled, he blew a thin line of smoke upwards. He also held the cigarette at the end of his fingertips, like a woman. I stared at this, wondering. I'd always smoked with the cigarette between my thumb and index finger, a bit like a soldier, not least because that way I could easily hide the cigarette in the palm of my hand, by flicking it backwards. I'd learned this from the older boys at school, when we smoked behind the bicycle sheds. I was utterly fascinated by these men's gestures and affectations.

By now, I was feeling drunk and didn't care much about anything. Alcohol was a fantastic thing, like instant sunshine. It made your cares and woes simply drop off your shoulders. The behaviour of my new friends was also changing, becoming more theatrical. Danny kept flicking his longish blonde hair, and Diarmuid was looking around, catching other men's eyes and holding their gaze. I started mimicking their behaviour and adopting their mannerisms, trying to be part of their game. They gave me a cigarette, and I held it up and out, like a girl.

For the first time in a long time, I felt as if I belonged

somewhere. The lads talked to me like a proper grown-up. There was lots of laughter, lots of jokes, and I was having the time of my life. Here I was, an eleven-year-old schoolboy, out drinking in town, with two mates, my equals. I related stories about my sisters, about Limerick, about school, about my dead father and my mother's strict regime, which I couldn't care less about as I raised my glass and cigarette. But, despite the heady excitement, I revealed nothing about my terrible experiences with men. That was far too shameful. I didn't want anything to put my new friendships at risk.

After the second drink, Danny said casually, 'We're staying down here for a while. Are you going home, or do you want to stay with us?' It was around nine o'clock by then, and I knew I should be getting home. But I also knew my mother would still be at The Lucky Lamp and, bolstered by my two scotches, I no longer cared. So what if Bernard stitched me up and I got a beating later. Right now, I was having the time of my life. These guys found me interesting enough to ask me to stay. But I had no money to buy them a drink back – maybe they were expecting that. But when I expressed my concern, Danny shrugged it off, saying it was fine. I was starting to feel quite attached to the lads.

After a while, Danny said that they needed the toilet, and asked did I know where the public ones were. I knew Limerick City well and was delighted to be able to be useful in my newfound role as their navigator. I was too intoxicated to question why they didn't use the pub toilets. I knew there were toilets on the Dock Road. I was used to cycling down there to pick up coal near Tedcastle's coal yard. We left the pub together, laughing and chatting amiably.

Once outside, the effects of the alcohol intensified. I felt quite light-headed by the time we reached the public toilets. I didn't need to use them, and Danny said, 'Stay outside and we'll be out in a minute.' I did as I was told and waited on the street corner. This was an old part of town and the small streets nearby were still cobbled. I watched men go into the toilet and not come out again, but I didn't think much of it. There were a few cars passing by, and it was getting dark and chilly, but I was content simply standing there, my head buzzing.

Ten minutes went by, then fifteen, then twenty. I began to get worried. And uncomfortable. As men went into the toilet, they stared at me strangely. Were Danny and Diarmuid all right? Had one of them got sick or fainted or something? I couldn't fathom where the hell they had gone to. I imagined the toilet was a Doctor Who-type Tardis. Maybe they'd zoomed off to another time zone altogether.

I gave it another five minutes. It was now almost half an hour since they'd left me outside. I finally went in. The scene that lay before me as I focused through the gloom sent my head reeling. The toilet was full of men, of all ages – youngsters, older men, middle-aged men – all hanging around the big drain that ran down the centre. There were six cubicles, three on either side, that also seemed to have men in them. The odd thing was that the men who were supposedly peeing into the drain weren't really peeing at all. They appeared to be staring at each other, with their penises in their hands.

At first, I felt a jolt of panic, unable to find the lads from Dublin. I went round the cubicles, first along one side, then the other. I pushed a half-open door of a cubicle, and there was Diarmuid, down on the floor on his knees, performing oral sex on another man.

I turned away at this sight, which reminded me of my own sickening experiences. At the drain in the middle, two men masturbated each other. Then I noticed a very young boy, perhaps even younger than me, disappear into a cubicle with a fat, middle-aged man, who closed the door behind them. I saw another boy, around my own age, standing at the entrance of the toilet, his shirt unbuttoned, his head leaning back against the doorway, invitingly. I figured he was a lookout until an older man came in and they went off together into an empty cubicle. It became clear that it was a pickup point.

Finally, a cubicle opened, and Danny emerged with an older man in tow. The second man was buttoning up his fly, and Danny was smoothing down his hair. They were talking, standing quite close to each other. The man handed Danny something, which he quickly pocketed.

I was utterly bewildered that such a thing was going on in a public place. Until then, my encounters had been furtive, shrouded in secrecy. I was still woozy from the drinks and struggling to think clearly. All the time I'd been gathering coal down the yard, I'd no idea what was going on just a short distance away.

I didn't know what to do. Should I go or stay? Should I say something to my new friends? Somehow, it didn't seem like a smart idea. I decided to go back outside, to the corner where I had been standing in the first place. I wondered if they had known about this place or come across it by sheer coincidence. Cars were driving past and slowing down. I realised then that they were looking at me, running their creepy eyes up and down me in the same way Aidan did. I was trying to puzzle it all out when Danny suddenly appeared in front of me.

'Diarmuid's on the ground, with a man's langer in his mouth,' I blurted out, unable to contain myself.

'Yes, that's what we did in Dublin,' said Danny, coolly. 'We made a lot of money on the docks to survive. It's what we do.'

I stared at him, open-mouthed. Danny saw my confusion and explained that he and Diarmuid liked to take drugs, cannabis in particular, and they needed to do this kind of thing to get money for them. I didn't know anything much about drugs at the time.

I had stumbled across something that was way beyond my years and felt badly out of my depth. I wanted to go home. Diarmuid was now back on the pavement with us. I looked at them with fresh eyes. These men, who had seemed so friendly, were openly telling me they were into drugs and willingly did peculiar things with men for money to pay for dope.

I shuddered at the thought of Aidan and his unsavoury gang. I thought about the rape in his car. I never wanted to go through that again, not for all the money in the world.

'Look at you,' Danny said, clearly picking up on my discomfort. 'Look at the holes in your shoes, look at your clothes, you could do with some cash.'

I looked down at my ropey old trainers, my frayed hand-me-down jeans and my cheap tatty jacket – I saw what he meant. 'You could make some money, you know. If you stay with us, we could help you make some. You'd like that, wouldn't you?' he said.

Danny had an easy charm about him, and he made what he was proposing sound like the most normal thing in the world. I wanted to please him, to gain his approval. And he was right, my clothes were grubby. I was a mess. He was offering me a way to make some money. I could buy decent clothes. I could be like him. I began to feel tempted. I had no understanding at that time of the process of sexualisation I had undergone by the grooming of Aidan and Sean.

Danny explained that the exact spot where I was standing on the street corner was the place to be picked up. 'If you stand around on any street corner in the docklands' area, you're for sale. Didn't you realise that, John?'

How the hell would I have realised that?

'But I'm not for sale,' I protested.

'Yes, I know,' said Danny soothingly, 'but you could be, y'know. And sooner than you think. We could actually make you five pounds tonight in a few minutes. And your mother need never know anything about it.'

Five pounds! This was serious money indeed. Much more tempting than the fifty pence I'd earned from Aidan, or the hard-earned pound from his pals. I couldn't believe it. But I'd seen what was happening inside in the toilets, and these guys knew what they were talking about.

Danny was focusing on me, at his most persuasive, while Diarmuid was hovering about restlessly, shifting from foot to foot, making eye contact with men as they came and went from the toilet. It was quite dark and I had to decide what to do next.

'It's your choice, John, you know that.' Danny placed his arm round my shoulder, comfortingly. He smelled good and was so far removed from the smelly, ugly men who were part of my life. 'You can make a fiver tonight, just like that,' he repeated, snapping his fingers for emphasis. 'But if you tell your mother, we'll be kicked out on the streets. And you wouldn't want that, would you?'

He was right. These were my new friends. Danny looked at me intently in the dim yellow light. He had the measure of me – he knew I was a ripe cherry, ready for the picking. 'Come on, John. Let's hang around and see. Come inside the door there' – he pointed to the entrance of the red-brick toilets – 'and we'll stand around you, and if anyone comes in, we'll talk to them.'

What did I have to lose that I hadn't already lost over the past three years? Danny was offering to protect me. It was what I had always wanted – an older man, a father figure to look out for me. When I had needed protection, that night on the doorstep, with Aidan waiting for me at the end of the road, the trusted adult who answered the door had failed me. Unwittingly, my father had failed me, in dying when I was a baby. Now, at this crucial moment in my life, I was easily led, lured by the promise of protection and an easy fiver.

Danny moved towards the door, followed by Diarmuid. I made up my mind. In that moment, I trusted them and, though my trust would soon be shattered, it would be a long time before I would be freed from their dangerous grip.

A shiver ran through me as I stood in the doorway of the public toilet. Diarmuid stood on one side of me, Danny on the other. He whispered advice in my ear: 'Don't kiss them. Never kiss them. All you have to do is go into the cubicle with them, just rub their cock for them until they're done – bring a bit of tissue paper with you and we'll get the money for you.'

A middle-aged man came in the toilet door, weaving slightly, and headed for the drain without looking at us. I held my breath until he'd passed by. I noticed Danny and Diarmuid try to establish eye contact with him, but he was too drunk to notice.

Next thing, the Dubliners looked at each other

significantly and then led me into one of the cubicles where they demonstrated what I should do. I didn't know where to look. Danny was talking to me all the while, like a friendly teacher explaining a biology class. 'Now this part' – he showed me the top of his penis – 'this is especially sensitive. The faster you make them finish, the quicker you get your money.' Desperate to please and still feeling drunk, I obeyed them when they asked me to demonstrate it.

Danny said, 'That's very good, that'll get them going,' and they laughed. I joined in out of pure nervousness. Danny zipped up his fly and we left the cubicle. He made it all seem perfectly straightforward, almost clinical. I didn't feel bullied or threatened like the other occasions, and there was the sweetening promise of five whole pounds at the end of it.

As I stood by the toilet entrance, flanked by the two lads, I imagined exactly what I would buy with the money: a pair of brown brogues, my very own new shoes. If anyone asked me where they came from, I'd say, 'Oh, I was down by the docks and I picked up loads of coal from Tedcastle's and sold it to people door to door.'

Danny broke into my reverie. 'The client will come in,' he whispered, while men in the toilet masturbated each other only a few feet away, 'and he'll size up who's available.' I looked over to the other side of the drain. Another young boy, about my age, stood with an older guy, probably Danny's age. I could see how the game worked. A 'client' came up and whispered in the older man's ear. Then the young boy was led away to the cubicle with the client, leaving the older man on guard outside the closed door, until the business was done.

A man came in and stood by us at the front door. He was bald and stockily built, like a rugby player. He appraised me quickly, then gazed around the toilet, before returning his gaze to me again. I was being sized up, like a piece of meat on a slab, and I felt a flush of humiliation. Sensing imminent business, Danny moved in front of me, and the man and Danny drew up to each other, eyeball to eyeball.

The man cocked his head and raised his eyebrow, looking pointedly at Danny, then nodding at me.

'He's with us,' Danny said in a low voice. 'I'll talk to you outside a sec.'

They disappeared outside, leaving me standing next to Diarmuid. I felt very frightened now that it was actually going to happen. I looked up at Diarmuid and he winked at me, which made me feel slightly better. I thought to myself, this is completely different to the Aidan situation. They are selling me, but they are protecting me at the same time. I thought again about my shoes.

Danny and the man came back into the toilet, and Danny bent down and whispered in my ear. 'He's a nice man, you go in with him, and there's a fiver after. All you have to do is wank him off.'

Without saying a word, the man turned and walked towards one of the cubicles. I was pushed forward by Danny and followed the man inside. He closed the door and locked it. It had filthy white tiles and red brick walls inside and there was a pungent smell of stale urine. A bare lightbulb dangled from the ceiling.

The man leaned back against the door and opened his zipper. For a second, I wanted to bolt for it. I reminded myself that I'd volunteered to come in here, I'd agreed to do this, and I just had to get on with it. The man gestured to the filthy seat, which had no lid. I sat on the toilet.

The air in the cubicle soon filled with the smell of his beery breath. Although he looked like a tough rugby player, he was well dressed in good quality clothes, and I wondered briefly if he'd mind if his stuff went over his leather shoes. As I got on with the job, I wondered how long it would take. I didn't notice if he had a wedding ring on or not, as his hands were in his trouser pockets. Danny had told me to look for their wedding rings; if they had one, they were more guilty, so you could get more money from them.

Finally, he finished up, and his white stuff spurted out all over my shirt and the toilet wall behind. He took out a large, ironed white handkerchief from his jacket to wipe himself off. In my innocence, I expected that he would clean me up, too, and felt hurt when he did not conduct this courtesy. I had a lot to learn.

I turned and pulled off some toilet roll and mopped my shirt. He turned round, opened the door and walked out. I followed and watched him go over to Danny. They went outside together again. Now that it was over, I felt let down and upset. I should have known better than to expect some thanks from the client. The circumstances may have been changed but this was just as sordid as anything that had happened me before – it was no different, no matter what I had told myself.

I wandered over to Diarmuid who was still standing by the door. He asked how it went. I shrugged and held back my tears. Danny returned, looking very pleased with himself. 'You did well,' he said glowingly.

'Did I?' I asked, trying to be cool. 'He shot his stuff all over me but didn't wipe it up.'

'"Cum",' said Danny. 'The white stuff is called "cum". You can't expect him to do that. After all, you're doing a job here: he's the client, the customer, and you're serving him, so it's all part of the service.'

I took this in, but I still felt unsettled by what had happened. 'So, where's the money?' I asked.

'Ah,' said Danny, ever the diplomat, 'we usually stay down for an hour or two to make enough money. Listen, we've heard there's some other toilets near here, and that's where we're going next.'

Seeing my face drop, Danny bundled me out of the door, with Diarmuid following, and we all headed off down the road. I fell silent. The bubble had burst, and I felt sulky and tired. I was also starting to feel nauseous, as the effects of the drink wore off. I just wanted to go home now, and it was well after ten o'clock. The reality of the trouble I'd be in was dawning. Danny, being the sensitive one, felt my change of mood as we drew up outside another docklands pub.

'Tell you what,' he said brightly, 'time for a little something.'

We entered the dingy bar, which seemed full of dockers, down-and-outs and strange-looking people. I didn't like this place, it felt dangerous to me, but the Dubliners seemed quite relaxed about it. I soon had another drink in my hand. And they gave me one of their special hand-rolled cigarettes, which tasted different to anything I had smoked before. It made my head feel light, and the heavy pounding of my heart abated for a while.

But I felt out of my depth – what had started off as a fun evening had turned serious and sordid. This pub was a sleazy dump with a heavy atmosphere, unlike the first place, which was glamorous by comparison. How was I going to get away from these guys tonight?

Much as I wanted to, I couldn't walk out. If I wasn't careful, I would get sucked into something like I had with Aidan, and I might not be able to get out again. I looked up at Danny and Diarmuid and wondered what on earth I was doing with them. Danny, on the other hand, remained upbeat, as if nothing out of the ordinary was unfolding.

'Look, it's OK,' he reassured me. 'We're here to help you, and you'll get your money soon enough.'

I sipped my drink, enjoying the burning sensation at the back of my throat and the numbing sensation that quickly followed. As I drank on, I relaxed more, and the mood picked up. Danny and Diarmuid were my minders, I told myself. They weren't forcing me into anything, I was making my own choices.

When I look back now, I recognise the cruel dynamic that was being skilfully played out. Danny instinctively knew just how vulnerable I was and was masterfully manipulating this to his own ends. I was desperate to have an adult in whom I could trust, and he was offering me his trust by making me feel that, for the first time, I could be the master of my own fate. I was an open target, who did not know how to protect myself against would-be abusers. As the evening progressed, I was taken in by Danny's easy charm, my tongue loosened from the alcohol. I found myself confiding about the past abuses: Aidan, his seedy mates, Garda McEvoy.

Danny's eyes widened as I revealed the catalogue of woes. 'Poor chicken,' he said, 'of course that was terrible, really awful. But this is different, isn't it? You're choosing to do this. And anyway' – he ruffled my hair affectionately – 'you're going to get some proper money this time, not just some skanky old fifty pence.'

Boy, but was he good. He knew exactly what buttons to press. This was exactly how I had been reasoning it out in my young mind. Yes, I had a choice, and by going in with the Dubliners, I was making the choice to no longer be just a random victim. Deep down, I felt that if I could convince myself of this, however bogus it was, then perhaps the consequences would be easier to bear.

Danny smiled and I smiled back. I finished my drink and felt much more reassured. Even Diarmuid, who seldom spoke, looked warmly at me and winked again.

After another scotch and red, I found myself confiding in them about the rape. I'd never told a living soul, not even confessed to God or a priest, but now I revealed the full horror of being ripped to shreds, of how I had bled for weeks afterwards.

Danny nodded sympathetically. 'Yes, yes,' he said, 'it hurt me as well the first few times. I know exactly what you mean.' He put his arm round me, and tears sprung into my eyes. He knew what I meant, he understood. He'd been there, too. This revelation was like gold dust to me. Danny reassured me that I was all right and that my body was very resilient, even 'down there', and that I would heal very well in time.

I cannot describe the enormous relief I felt at that moment. For the past six months, I had lived every day with the mounting fear that some horrible disease was growing through my body. At last, I had spoken about it to a grown-up, and they had reassured me that my worst fears were unfounded.

'Listen to me, honey,' said Danny, 'I'm won't allow anyone to do anything to you that you don't want, y'hear?'

I nodded. Danny got out a tissue and wiped away my tears. 'You do just what you want, and we will help you,' he said. 'I'll look after you, we both will, won't we Diarmuid?'

Diarmuid nodded and winked again at me. I felt as if a weight had been lifted from my shoulders.

'Come on, let's go and find another toilet,' said Danny, knocking back the rest of his drink and slamming the glass down on the bar.

I copied him, feeling like a cowboy in a western movie. Diarmuid joined in, and all three of us laughed at our antics as we headed into the night.

13

The Tricks of the Trade

This is how the prostitution and pimping scene worked in the 1970s in Limerick City. The main activity ran from the public toilets under Sarsfield Bridge (right in the centre of town) along the quays to the toilet at the bottom of Lower Mallow Street, and out along the Dock Road past the entrance to the harbour, ending roughly at Alphonsus Street. In all, it was less than a mile.

Some of the pubs across the road from the harbour were regular pick-up places for the female prostitutes. We tended to use the two public toilets. On any evening, from dusk onwards, there would be about fifteen prostitutes, huddled in small groups of four or five.

One group worked down at the end of the cobbled Alphonsus Street. On O'Curry Place, two or three women had their pitch. Others were in the pubs, or down laneways servicing their clients. Others huddled in groups; young and middle-aged, thin and fat, all selling their bodies. Most were there for two reasons: to feed their alcoholism and to feed their families. Some women were pimped by their husbands. I knew one or two girls my own age who were being pimped by their fathers. One man had three or four of his daughters on the game on the Dock Road at any one time. There were six or seven, sometimes up to ten, male prostitutes, all young and most well under age.

Nightly, I would go straight down to The Penthouse with Danny and Diarmuid. We'd have a couple of drinks there, then go and check out toilet number one. The drink, and the special cigarettes, which I found out had hash in them, really loosened me up and helped me shed my fears and inhibitions. After spending time 'working' there, we would go to the rough docks' pub and have two more drinks, then go on to the second toilet to 'work'. This was the routine, and the guys believed it worked well. I didn't question it.

The second toilet at the other end of the Dock Road was also red brick but had brighter lighting, especially when we entered from the street. On that first night, I had 'serviced' a second client in one of the cubicles before heading home and hiding my hard-earned fiver under my mattress.

Usually, at this toilet, a couple of young boys hung around the door. Cars cruised up and then down again. It was possible to figure out from the road whether it was worth parking and walking over or not. It wasn't possible to see the door of the toilet from the bridge above, so clients either came down by foot and looked in the door or brought their car round and parked outside, then walked in.

From that first night in The Penthouse, a new pattern of life emerged for me. I slipped into a daily routine with the Dubliners which would go on for over two years, until I was almost fourteen. I would go to school, tired, hungover and grumpy. I would be argumentative and provocative, get shouted at, even hit or caned. My attitude was aggressive and uncooperative; being at school just seemed a ridiculous facade, a bizarre cover for my extraordinary and secretive 'real' life, which was being lived on the wild side, every night.

I failed to study or even do homework – it seemed irrelevant – and, anyway, I was often too hungover to concentrate. I would come home, often having skipped classes or, sometimes, mitched school for the whole day. I would make some tea, then set off around seven or eight for an evening with Danny and Diarmuid.

I have no idea what my mother thought we were up to. Despite my initial fears, she was not bothered by my going out with the guys and never asked questions. In fact, during this time, her behaviour towards me improved, and all seemed well on the surface.

That first week, I came home with twenty pounds, which was a small fortune to me. On one level, I felt proud of myself, to have endured what I did every night. It was very tough going, and I had earned my money. I went and bought my pair of top-of-the-range brogues. I was proud of them, too.

Mammy noticed them and quizzed me. I told her that the Dubliners had got themselves some casual bar work and had bought me the brogues as a thank you for taking them to the pubs. They had teased me at home quite openly about the state of my shoes, so she seemed to buy this explanation, which both surprised and relieved me.

I had gradually got used to what the clients wanted me to do. I didn't want to do it – it still felt disgusting – but I was getting better at it. I was learning, too, how to be a people-pleaser, adopting the 'camp' mannerisms I witnessed and honing my soliciting skills. I began to learn what would make men 'come' quickly and how to avoid the mess covering my clothes.

Meanwhile, the Dubliners were continuing to supply me with the attention I so badly craved. I was like a dry sponge, needy and desperate to soak up anything that was vaguely suggestive of love or affection. The guys would sweep me out of the house, having charmed my mother and made her laugh. Once we were walking down town, as a trio, they would pass me cigarettes, then buy me drinks. I was being both seduced and groomed by them. I was their 'talent', and they were training me up, like a circus poodle, to perform my nightly tricks.

I was willing and eager to learn, willing to do what they wanted because, aside from wanting to please them, and thereby secure their attentions, at the back of my mind was the lingering fear that they might tell my mother what I was up to. I felt very vulnerable: this pair knew the full story of my sordid past. And they were subtly playing on it, using their knowledge and my fear to keep me in line.

I had told Danny and Diarmuid where Aidan lived. One day, soon after their arrival, I returned from school to find them waiting for me, looking smug. As I made some toast, Danny sauntered into the kitchen. 'Well, John, you won't be having any more visits from your tormentor,' he said.

'What?'

'Squealed like a pig, he did,' said Diarmuid, joining in, which was rare for him. I swung round, toast in hand, my eyes wide.

'Yeah, that's right,' Danny confirmed, sensing my amazement. 'Aidan won't be coming for you any more.'

Apparently, they had gone and knocked on his door, and when he'd opened it, Diarmuid had lured him out on some pretext or other and then threatened him. They had both told Aidan what they would do to him, in no uncertain terms, if he ever came near me again. I hadn't seen Aidan at all since the guys had arrived, though I had wondered what would happen if he found out about my new life.

But, after the guys' visit, he never did come and get me again, so whatever they had said to him obviously frightened him off. No doubt he was soon busy grooming some other unsuspecting child. But I was very relieved that he seemed finally to be out of my life.

I didn't understand it at the time but, in effect, a change of ownership had taken place. I had been handed from one master to another, to do my tricks for a new audience, somewhere else. Ironically, the fact that the Dubliners had sorted out Aidan made me more loyal to them, just as it put me further into their debt – something they would play on as time went on, to my detriment. They were my pimps, and I had become their rent boy.

One night, during that second week, we were walking to toilet number one, having had our couple of warm-up drinks. Danny once again brought up the possibility of giving clients oral sex. The very thought of this made me sick, and Danny knew it. I couldn't believe he was mentioning it again. On the first night with the second client, I'd refused to perform oral sex, and it was accepted by them that I'd never be asked to do so. Danny looked as friendly as always, but a familiar hard edge had come into his voice.

'Look, John, it's easy to do,' he argued as he started to describe what was involved, ignoring my protests. When he finished, he stared at me, unblinkingly. Not only was his voice changing, his manner was becoming more dominating. I realised I couldn't win this argument. Danny was stronger than me, his will was fierce, and I could see he was determined I was going to do it. My stomach churned. 'Why not have a go tonight, John? We'll be here for you, just like always.'

The stakes of our dangerous, seedy enterprise had just got higher. But, although I felt powerless in the face of

Danny's intentions, I still could not agree. After what had happened me before, when my friend's older brother had tried to force me into oral sex, I knew just how sickening it was. I held out, refusing point blank to do it.

At the end of the second week, I found I had less money from Danny than usual. When I asked why this was, he said, 'Some weeks are good, some are bad.' Then he turned up the heat. 'Of course, if you did blow jobs properly, you could earn more.'

Ah, so that was the problem. My money had been docked. I hadn't delivered what they had promised the punter. I was being punished. In hindsight, I know that I was only being given a small portion of what I was 'earning' anyway – there's no doubt they were making a tidy penny from the fruits of my labour, which they squandered on drugs and booze. But, at the time, I was oblivious, satisfied to settle for my nightly fiver.

I learned the hard way to service the clients as they wanted, my need to please Danny overriding my revulsion at the sexual acts I was being forced to perform. And, ultimately, the cash, which afforded me cigarettes and new clothes, provided a buffer against the reality of what was unfolding.

Some time later, Danny upped the stakes yet again. 'You know, John, you can earn more money if you go in their car with them.' Once again, I froze. In a car? He had to be joking. We were standing at the bar in The Penthouse, having our second drink before hitting the first toilets of the evening. Diarmuid nodded in agreement.

I hated the thought of being in a car, after my horrific experience with Aidan. The possibility of being raped again seemed all too real, and I was terrified.

'Don't worry, we'll check them out for you,' said Danny, eager to sweet-talk me but barely concealing his nice-guy-to-nasty tendency. 'You know, John, you've done all these hand jobs and blow jobs with us and got paid for it, and I'd hate your mother to find out . . .'

I was being blackmailed. Yet again, I was swimming way out of my depth. We were walking along a dark pavement towards the toilet, with Danny beside me and Diarmuid trailing behind.

'No.' I stood firm. 'I won't do it.'

I felt a sharp pain in my kidneys, like I'd been kicked by the hind legs of a donkey. I fell to my knees. Then another kick came, to the same spot, and searing pain shot through my body. A trainer now dug into my stomach, winding me completely. I doubled over on the pavement, virtually throwing up, and struggled to get my breath. I felt as if my kidneys must be on the end of Diarmuid's boots. They dragged me up to my feet to face them.

'Listen to me, John, you little prick,' sneered Diarmuid, breathing into my face, 'you haven't got much fucking choice.' The masks were off. I saw the true men behind them. It was the first beating they gave me, but it wouldn't be their last.

As I begged them to stop, Danny quickly reverted to Mr Nice Guy mode. 'John, John, listen, we're yer friends . . . hey?

We got rid of that ugly fuck, didn't we? We're in it together now.' He put his arm round me, trying to cajole me. I wanted to spit in his face.

I felt totally intimidated. Yet again, I was being cajoled and threatened, all at once. When it came down to it, they were no different to Aidan.

Danny could read my fear. He knew when to turn on the charm, when to toughen up. 'Look,' he began, 'aren't we after making some money here? Things are gonna get better for you from now on, I promise . . .'

He wiped my tears away, but I shrugged him off. It was too much, too fucking much. The suicidal thoughts that had plagued me when I was curled up in bed after a degrading session with Aidan or one of his perverted cronies came flooding back. No one could be trusted, everyone wanted something, and even if they seemed nice, they never, ever were.

I wanted to lie on the pavement and howl. I wanted to take a running jump off a bridge into the river – anything to escape the knowledge that Danny and Diarmuid would get their way. But I had nowhere to run. It was the same as ever: fooled, then betrayed, I was being pushed to do things that I didn't want to do but felt I had no way out of it. I was worn down, utterly divested of any morsel of self-esteem, locked into a cycle of fear, violence, manipulation. Reluctantly, inevitably, I gave in.

'All you have to do is get in the car and do what the client wants,' said Danny brightly, as if it was the easiest thing in the world. 'If he wants you to go down on him, then you'll do that. He'll expect full oral sex.'

I was promised five pounds per job, which was far better than a fiver for a whole night. I thought, If I end up at the bottom of the river, who will care? I wouldn't be missed. So, when the time came, I got into a car with a client, a cream Renault 18. I was absolutely terrified and, as often happened at such times, my legs shook involuntarily. Danny had whispered I'd be OK, that he'd checked him out.

As I got into the car, I saw that the middle-aged driver had a large set of black rosary beads hanging off his front mirror. He also had a picture of the Sacred Heart and a model of the pontiff on his windscreen. A devout Catholic, obviously. I saw a ring glinting on his left hand, so he was married, too. Hypocrite.

Danny had made it clear that my job was to put this man at his ease, yet I found it hard to hide my awkwardness, let alone be pleasant to him. A fiver a trick, a fiver a trick. The thought kept pulsing through my brain. A fiver a trick. That surely would make it worthwhile.

The man drove out into the countryside, and soon I was utterly lost. 'We're going to a place where we're going to be safe,' he said, 'where nobody will come upon us.' At these words, my heart started racing. What if he cut my throat or strangled me, who would know or care? Would I care?

I eventually recognised Beigh Castle, a well-known landmark outside Limerick, which, it transpired, was a favourite spot with this man. In a bid to quell my nerves, I tried to strike up a conversation. More than anything, I didn't want to give him any reason to get angry. In a way, I felt like I was defusing a bomb, having to be very careful what I did or said in case everything exploded in my face.

He wanted oral sex, but he didn't want to have it in the car. Maybe he was worried about the mess, which his wife might notice. Maybe he felt guilty being sucked off by a child under the gaze of the Sacred Heart and the pontiff. Who knows?

He got out and went round to the back of the car and leaned against the boot. I followed. He'd obviously done this before. It was pitch black and the wind was howling. We were quite near the Shannon River and I wondered, briefly, if I might end up in there by the end of the night. He unzipped his fly and pulled his pants down. I had to conduct the dirty business on my knees, in the dark, on the soggy turf. I knelt in this humiliating position, in the dark and cold, while he pleasured himself.

As the man cleaned himself off and zipped himself up, I vomited on the ground, purging myself of his revolting stuff. I didn't care what he thought, despite Danny's instructions to be pleasing and demure. But it didn't matter anyway – he didn't see me. He was already back in the warmth of the car, eager to get out of there.

I cleaned myself up the best I could and got back into the car. 'You'll be OK,' he said as he started up the engine. 'Open the window, I don't want you to be sick in the car.' Glad of the air, I duly opened the window and looked out into the black night.

'I feel guilty now about having been with you,' he said in a quiet voice, 'but I've been doing this for years . . . I can't seem to stop.'

I was amazed by his confession. As my stomach churned, he told me of how his secret life made him feel anxious and guilty, but he couldn't give it up. He had a wife, three kids at college and a pressured job. Doing this was his only real release and pleasure.

Yeah, I thought, your pleasure but my pain. I could see the crucifix swinging from the rear-view mirror. It seemed to mock us both. If Christ suffered for our sins, as the priests insisted, then he must spend every second of eternity in mortal agony.

'I've got to bring you back to your guys now,' he said gently, my barely veiled disgust obviously stoking his newfound guilt. On the way out, I had played the game I was being taught to play, but on the way back, I was too sick to continue with the pretence.

Danny was waiting for me where the car finally pulled in outside the toilet. 'You'll be OK,' he whispered as I hurried past, head down. He came over to join me as I stood by the outside wall. 'Look' – he tried to sound placatory – 'the only reason you were sick is that you took it way too far into the back of your mouth. I told you to take it and suck it from the side – they don't even notice.'

John Devane

What I noticed was how he didn't give a shit about how I was feeling, not for a moment. I told him I felt sick, that I hated it. 'You'll get used to it,' he said flatly.

Diarmuid was alongside us now and he winked at me. 'You did good,' he said. It was a rare word from Diarmuid, so things must be desperate.

'How about a drink?' said Danny. In truth, I was dying for a drink, as by now I had developed a serious taste for it. And I knew the hash that would come would block out all sense of harsh reality. The lads were not only teaching me to degrade myself for a fiver, they were teaching me to drink like a fish. In later years, I calculated that, at eleven years of age, I was consuming around twenty units of spirits a week.

After our usual second pub stop, we moved on to the next toilet. Business was fairly slow and we made an early night of it. On the way home, Danny handed me a fiver, as always. By my calculations, it should have been a fiver for the job in the car and a fiver for the rest of the evening. 'Why isn't it ten pounds?' I asked, incensed.

'Ah,' said Danny, smoothly, 'your man in the car didn't pay me enough – he said he didn't have as much money as he thought he had.' I was incandescent but also quite pissed by now. I shot dagger looks at Danny. 'It'll be better next time,' he said.

Like hell, I thought, as I staggered home wearily.

14

The Double Life

Boy, did I learn to lie. I had to in order to survive. A web of lies was spun, and I was like the obedient money fly caught in the middle of it, providing cash for two greedy spiders who had total control over my body and my life. For the next four or five months I learned how to live a double life, as I absorbed all the tricks of the trade. The Dubliners told me to tell my mother and brother that they had got two night-time jobs as barmen and that I was helping out and earning some pocket money. That would explain where the funds for my expanding new wardrobe were coming from.

My new wardrobe didn't consist of sensible things to wear. It was designed to pull in the punters. I was taught that the clients liked tight white jeans, in particular, tucked into cowboy boots, as they displayed you to your best advantage. I had picked up the 'camp' mannerisms of the Dubliners, flicking my hair, pouting, wiggling my hips, making eye contact and being suggestive.

At home, Mammy failed to pay attention to the transformation. Perhaps she believed it was teen fashion, not high camp, and as long as I was with the Dubliners, I was fine.

At school, things continued to decline. I was expelled from the Christian Brothers' school not long after the Dubliners came into my life. The discipline imposed on me by the teachers only made me more determined to challenge it. It gave me an opportunity to channel my pent-up anger. Without being conscious of it, I was doing so in a controlled, safe environment. I had rules to break, a structure that provided a conduit for my raw, unprocessed emotions.

Outside the classroom, there were no rules to break. There were no structures to kick against. Outside was a chaotic, free-for-all jungle. How can you kick against something that is bigger than you but impossible to grasp? The shadowy world I occupied was not visible to the ordinary eye. To all intents and purposes, it did not exist. Men filled the pews at mass on Sunday, headed obediently on annual pilgrimages and retreats. The vast majority of them were good men, fathers, brothers, husbands. But if you lined them up in an identity parade alongside the men who furtively entered those toilets at night, who among them could be correctly identified as a paedophile, a child abuser?

In school, I had an identity. I was a trouble maker, an upstart, a boy who gave cheek to his teachers and who was probably the bane of their lives. Outside, there was nothing to separate me from the other young boys who entered the infested cubicles and provided a brief pleasure to their clients, who would not recognise them the following day and, if they did, would hastily look in the other direction.

Most of the time I was in school, I was simply too tired, distracted and hungover to give a damn. My concentration was limited, my sleep pattern all over the place. One day, I took a bicycle belonging to a fellow pupil, because I wanted to get home fast. Although I returned it to school the following day, the boy had reported it missing, and I was accused of stealing it. Although I argued that I'd only borrowed it, my protests didn't wash, and I was expelled. When my mother heard the news, she was understandably furious.

Later, I was accepted, with some difficulty, at a new school, St Munchin's. Here, I had to accept a tougher regime. At first, I actually fared quite well. I hoped it might offer me a new beginning but, in time, the gulf between my daytime life and my nighttime activities began to take its toll once more. Within that strict framework, I could once again kick over the traces. What was the worst that could happen to me: detention, suspension, expulsion? I was losing all respect for authority, and this real world in which I belonged was giving way to the dangerous world that beckoned me every night. My old antics returned. I became rude and challenging to teachers, sometimes even aggressive. I had endless warnings, reprimands and detentions.

Despite these volatile tendencies, I remained prey to older bullies. My fine features and slender frame marked me out from my tougher-looking peers. I wasn't as meek as I looked and would always fight back. But there was one bully who was impossible to take on, especially when his bullying was done with impunity in the classroom.

This teacher had a fearsome reputation for discipline, imposed through violent methods. One day, he stormed into the classroom in his usual aggressive manner. We used to sit in two-seater desks and, on this occasion, he noticed that three of us were sitting at the same desk. Jack, one of the pupils, had joined the two of us at our desk for a chat. Unlike some of the other incidents that I'd been involved in, this was nothing serious, yet the teacher bellowed at us, demanding to know which one of us was sitting at the wrong desk.

Jack put his hand up. 'I am, sir, I came up to get something.'

But the teacher was not convinced. Doubtless, he'd had his fill of my antics, and this gave him an opportunity to impose some serious discipline, his way.

'You're not the wrong one,' he said to Jack. 'Devane is.' He strode over to where we were sitting, lifted me up by the shoulders and pulled me over the desk. He then threw me from one wall of the prefab classroom to the other. I saw stars when I banged my head on the metal storage heater. Next, he took me out to the cloakroom, where he bounced me off the wall then punched me in the mouth. I was cut and bleeding by this stage but he was still in a frenzy. Finally, to my horror, he hung me by my clothes from a hook, with my back facing the wall, and left me there for the remainder of the class.

This was a final humiliation. Nowhere was safe. Even within the secure environment of a school it was possible for violence to overflow. Any lingering interest I had in furthering my education disappeared that day, and I simply went through the motions. Time seemed to crawl by as I endured each lesson, my mind elsewhere, usually reliving the events of the previous night or dreading what the oncoming one held in store.

This crazy double life was becoming increasingly difficult to sustain and, a couple of weeks later, the headmaster asked me why I wasn't paying attention properly in class. I told him about the unmerciful beating I had received. In those days, corporal punishment was meted out freely to impose discipline and was accepted by many teachers and parents as a natural aspect of school life. This was usually administered within limits, resulting in stinging hands or a jerked ear. What had happened in that cloakroom would be recognised as an assault today and would make headlines.

The headmaster refused to take me at my word and claimed that no teacher in his school would do anything like that. I was warned to knuckle down and pay attention to my lessons if I wanted to continue attending the school.

This incident, and the headmaster's response, so enraged

me that I soon lost all sense of boundaries at school. From that point on, I let loose: throwing dusters in the classroom, unscrewing teacher's seats so that they would fall off, and unscrewing lightbulbs to launch at unsuspecting passers-by.

What my school pals and the teachers saw was a boy hell-bent on self-destruction. What they didn't see was the other side of my identity: child prostitute, performing sexual acts by night.

I had a couple of girlfriends at this time. Even though I was being groomed by the lads from Dublin, I was as shy and excited as any boy of my age when I was in the presence of girls. It was all very innocent, a peck on the cheek, or a kiss with closed mouths – a far cry from my alternative life on the streets.

The pressure of keeping it all together was enormous. By now, suicidal thoughts were commonplace, especially when I woke up in the morning after a night 'on the job', hungover and full of self-loathing. I often contemplated how I would take my life and considered stockpiling painkillers so I could take an overdose.

It had only taken a few months of careful grooming to get me to where they wanted me, and they tightened their grip even further by telling me I'd be sent to a borstal, or reformatory school as it was called then, if I was caught by the gardaí.

*

One night, in the docks' toilets, a middle-aged man came in. There was nothing in particular to set him apart from the others of his type: he looked well-heeled, a thickset chubby man, with blue eyes and wispy grey hair, combed back. He was wearing a bulky anorak, collar up against the cold night outside. I assumed he was just the usual secretly gay married man.

Danny quickly did the deal, and I followed the man into the cubicle. He leaned back against the door, and I started to give him a oral sex, as instructed. At one point, he unzipped his jacket. I looked up to see his face. To my absolute horror, I saw the white collar, which his jacket had been concealing. A priest! I froze, utterly shocked. Nothing had prepared me for this. Priests were celibate. Everyone knew that they had given their lives to God and renounced worldly things like marriage and children. I served them at mass. I watched them transform bread into the body and blood of Jesus Christ. I still believed that this transformation took place each time I rang the bell and the congregation bowed their heads in respect. The statue of Our Lady Queen of Peace stood on our avenue, which had been named after her. If a priest was Christ's representative on earth, then she was this man's divine mother. What did she think, looking down on us, as I serviced him just the same as any other punter? He was impatient, intent on a swift surge of pleasure and a rapid departure. He was no different than any other person who came into those seedy toilets that night.

After it was over, my mind raced. It had all happened so

swiftly. Perhaps I'd mistaken the collar. No mistake. In time, this pathetic man of the cloth would become a regular of mine and of many of the other boys in the toilet.

After the trip out to Beigh Castle with the married Catholic father-of-three, I quickly got used to going out in cars, and it became a regular occurrence. Not surprisingly, though, the money I got for my troubles always stayed the same, despite promises to the contrary. I lived in the vain hope that the next time I wouldn't be short-changed.

One night, I was instructed to go on one such job. 'Blow job,' Danny whispered in my ear as I approached the car. No sooner had I sat into the car than I regretted it. My instincts, borne from bitter experience, were keenly honed by now, and I knew in my gut that trouble lay ahead. This man was middle-aged, as were the majority of them, and looked big and burly.

He was very drunk. The smell of alcohol in the car was overwhelming. As we drove into the night, my feelings of fear intensified. About a quarter of a mile from the toilets, he parked the car in the area near where the ships came in. Straight away, he launched himself at me and tried to pull me over the gear lever to where he was sitting in the driving seat. First he tried to kiss me. I was horrified and struggled to get away. But he held tight to my jacket. His face held an expression that I recognised well by now: lust-filled, with dead eyes. He was going to have me, his way, or no way. My antennae were on full alert. I was in deep trouble.

Furious at my rejection of his kiss, he threw me hard against the passenger door, then lunged at me and tried to turn me over in my seat. This rang loud warning bells, and I was determined he would not get his way.

'Turn over,' he shouted at me, blearily, pulling at my sleeve and trying to push me over.

'No.'

'What do you mean "No"?' he roared. 'Fucking turn over!'

I resisted and he punched me in the chest, winding me. He then lunged at me again, but this time to open the passenger door. He gave me a mighty shove and I fell out onto the hard cold ground. He leaned over and pulled the door shut, drunkenly shouting, 'You're not fucking worth it, you little fucking fag.' He fired up the engine, slammed the car into reverse and swung round, very nearly running me over.

It suddenly occurred to me that he would drive over me, such was the severity of his anger. And, sure enough, at that moment, he turned the car around again, in a swerving U-turn, and drove directly into my path. I had to roll over fast to avoid being caught under his wheels.

When I arrived back at the toilets, around an hour later, I was still very shaken. Danny and Diarmuid were annoyed that I'd lost the punter, and precious time. Time was money. Danny told me I wouldn't be paid for this particular job. By now his veneer of charm was paper thin.

Later that night, I would see this veneer slip even more. We had retired to the pub and, after a couple of drinks,

Danny pulled me past the bar into the toilet cubicle and said, 'I've taught you enough, now you show me what you've learned.' He was still angry with me about the lost client and wanted to punish me. I was forced to give him oral sex.

I had to learn the hard way that Danny was neither friend, nor mentor, but my pimp. To him, I was just goods – a product he could use and abuse, as it suited him.

15

Chicken

'Chicken' is the word in the trade for young male flesh, particularly young children's flesh. Having a virgin is a real speciality, worth money to the pimp. Within this circle, a look conveys meaning, a gentle nod as significant as a signal at an auction. Even in those pre-internet days, there was an effective information highway and a gallery of photographs.

During those first six months of being sold on the streets, I received a lot of repeat business. The Catholic father-of-three continued to choose me over the other boys on offer, and it was always the same routine out at Beigh Castle. Other men also came back for me. I began to know what they liked and how to please them. I learned how to engage in small talk and grew used to their flattery, which usually took place before business.

'You've got a beautiful arse in those white jeans,' they

would say and I would flirt back, pout my mouth, make them feel good about themselves. As soon as they had been serviced, there might be some more small talk but, mostly, they lost interest once the deed was done. None of them wanted to hang around the toilets longer than necessary.

I was getting good at the job. My growing popularity meant that I was becoming a good little earner for the Dubliners, who showed no signs of returning to their native city. Limerick was proving to be a lucrative alternative.

Sometimes I managed to make some money of my own, although it was usually at a price. One night, I got into a car with a client who had specified to Danny that he wanted a virgin.

'He's going to pay you a tenner,' said Danny, who was always at his most friendly when the price was high. Yeah, I thought, and what's he paying you? But I kept my thoughts to myself. Danny had a short fuse and it was dangerous to set him off. 'This punter wants someone young who hasn't done it before. Just play along. He's so drunk, he'll never know the difference.'

This was a large, heavy-set man with a huge beer belly. Danny was right, he was obviously drunk, and he drove slowly, jerkily out of town. The car turned this way and that. His breath reeked of alcohol and his speech was slurred – which was commonplace among these men. I often wondered if they had sons my own age and what they would do to a man who abused them in the same way as they now were abusing me. Not that I called it 'abuse' back then. It was work, he was a punter, and, as he drove into a lane beside a pub and a cement factory, a suitably remote place for his purposes, it was obvious that he wanted to relish the flesh of a young virgin boy in the privacy of his own car.

Eventually, he brought the car to an abrupt halt and switched off the headlights. In the complete darkness, I felt the familiar surge of fear. What if he had a knife? What if he was a psycho? Suddenly, he grabbed me with his large hands, pushed me back in my seat and flung himself across me. His huge beer belly flattened me and forced the breath from my body. It was obvious he was too drunk to ravish his 'virgin' and, after a few desultory attempts, all movement stopped. I realised, to my utter relief, that he had fallen unconscious.

With some difficulty, I rolled him off me. He was breathing heavily, sleeping off the effects of the night's drinking. There and then, I made the decision to rob him. I'd never done this before but, without the slightest twinge of guilt, I went through his pockets while he snored on his back with his mouth open. His wallet was crammed full of notes and credit cards. I took every last penny he had, including the cards. Then I whisked out his car keys from the ignition and popped them in my pocket. I began the long walk home, but this time I resolved not to go back to the docks.

As I walked, I counted the money in the wallet. Over seventy pounds, a small fortune. I pocketed the money. This was a rich victory. Let him sleep off his drunken binge and explain how he came to be stranded in a dark lane, minus his credit cards and car keys. Try explaining that to the guards. 'All I wanted to do was deflower a virgin boy, guard.' I laughed out loud at the thought as I threw his car keys over a high fence into the long grass. I was aware that I was committing a crime but, boy, did it seem justified.

When I saw Danny and Diarmuid again, I was careful not to tell them how things with the drunken punter had panned out. I knew by then that I had to keep that kind of 'free money' secret, and I stashed it under my mattress. I didn't feel bad about my subterfuge: I felt I was earning every single penny the hard way, so I damn well had the right to keep something for myself. I liked being able to buy stuff that I had always wanted, like good clothes and records, and I was becoming accustomed to having these things. Life on the streets was teaching me to be quite an artful dodger.

But I still felt utterly trapped. The threat of my mother finding out hung over me and that, combined with the threat of being sent to the dreaded borstal, was enough to keep me in line.

Meanwhile, they were always thinking up new ways to up their earnings through me, especially when trade was slow. They would set me up on a stool in The Penthouse, at the end of the bar, looking provocative in my white tight jeans and would then tout for business, which would be conducted in the toilets. I would have to perform the usual tricks. I don't know if they were using more drugs by now, and simply needed more money, or if they were just becoming more bold and confident over time. By now, I was deeply embroiled in the sordid world of rent-boy prostitution, performing sexual acts in an array of places, as they expanded my rent-boy repertoire.

One winter night, at the Dock Road pub we regularly frequented, some sailors came in. They were brutal-looking men, weather-beaten, scarred and stocky. I reckoned they were Eastern European. They worked on the trade ships that docked for three or four days at a time on the quayside over the road from the pub, and they came to get drunk and laid. Simple as that.

This pub attracted a wide range of prostitutes and, by now, I was on nodding acquaintance with these girls and women, as well as the other rent boys. There were often three or four 'women of the night' hovering around the bar, sometimes girls only a bit older than me, maybe fifteen or sixteen. The rent boys tended to be younger, starting at around nine or ten. The rough, horny sailors had a wide range of juvenile performers on show for their amusement.

Trade was slow this night. We'd done our usual route and had hardly pulled anyone. I was quietly relieved, but the guys were restless. And Danny, being Danny, was not going to give up that easily. I noticed he was chatting intently to some of the older women prostitutes. Eventually, he came back over to myself and Diarmuid. 'We're going to do some business up where the girls go,' he said in a whisper.

'Where's that?'

'You'll see – it'll be a bit of an adventure.'

I was feeling cold and tired and wanted an early night, but I knew that the glint in Danny's eyes meant money. After more drinks than usual, we swayed out of the pub. Some of the older women were in front, with sailors alongside them, arms round their waists. Danny, Diarmuid and I followed behind. I was quite drunk by this stage and hardly felt the cold wind as it whipped around my thin jacket collar.

We crossed the road, over to the docks, and came to the huge grey iron gates at the entrance. Danny went up ahead to talk to a guy near the dock gate. We soon filed through a little entrance gate, which was in the middle of the two huge gates. The guy sat there, reading his newspaper. He didn't look up.

Ahead of us was a vast expanse of concrete, with various dockside buildings and huts all around. All were in darkness, except the ship looming over us, prow first, straight ahead. I'd never seen a ship so large or so close up before, but my initial excitement quickly gave way to apprehension about what lay ahead.

The ship had Russian-style writing on the side and a foreign flag flying that I didn't recognise, with white and gold on it. A huge chain anchored it to the dockside. There were lights twinkling on board, smoke coming out of an enormous funnel somewhere, and two wooden gangways lined with ropes, jutting out from the side down to a bollard on the dock. It was around midnight now, and when I looked back towards the closed dock gates, it seemed ominously dark. The Dock Road was fairly quiet at that time of night. If nobody saw us arriving, nobody would come if things went horribly wrong.

My heart was thumping wildly as we walked up the gangplank. I whispered to one of the young women prostitutes, 'What's it like on a ship? Do they ever take off with you on it?'

She laughed good-naturedly and told me that we got thrown off before they departed, usually by the captain in the early hours. 'The sailors will pick up anyone they fancy,' she explained. 'Sometimes it'll be the girls, sometimes the boys, sometimes both – you never know what's going to happen.'

This didn't make me feel any better at all. But, before I could think about it further, I was led round the deck towards the bridge, and we all clattered down the steel rungs of a very narrow ladder that led into the crew's living quarters below deck. There was a room with a white metal table riveted to the floor and fixed seats round it.

It was full of men, chatting and swigging out of bottles, dressed in jeans and shirts. I was surprised they weren't wearing sailors' outfits, but the prostitute explained that they didn't wear them on shore leave when they liked to let their hair down. There were a mixture of officers and deckhands, about twenty in all, and they had obviously been partying for some time. I was handed a bottle of ice-cold vodka to swig from. It was rough-tasting and burned when it went down, but it numbed my senses further. A lot of the guys in the room were blond with blue eyes, rugged-jawed, thick-necked and muscular, with beefy arms.

I was told they were Russians, Poles, Latvians and Czechoslovakians. I had to stand, with the other prostitutes and rent boys, and display myself. I felt like a hunk of raw flesh on display in the butcher's window. Danny and Diarmuid moved around the room, chatting to the sailors, who were swigging back beer, vodka and whiskey straight from the bottle. I took some more vodka, to quell my nerves, but my young prostitute friend whispered in my ear I ought not to get too pissed, as I needed to keep my wits about me. I tried to heed her words, but I was nervous, and the bottle kept being passed to me.

Then one of the sailors came over to me and caught me by the wrist. He was a mountain of a man. Oh Lord, I thought, here we go. He led me to sleeping quarters behind the mess room, with rows of grey metal bunks nailed to the floor. It stank of stale sweat and cigarette smoke. Danny had gestured that I was to give this client a blow job, which I did. Afterwards, he threw me out of the bunkroom and fell asleep, snoring loudly.

As I returned to the party, another sailor grabbed my hand and pulled me into another bunk area on the other side of the mess room. This sailor wasn't as burly as the first one, but he was still a big man. He had wiry muscles and a thick neck. He wasn't interested in the normal course of business, either, as he quickly made his intentions clear, shaping one hand into a circle with his thumb and forefinger, then poking the index finger of the other hand through the hole in the middle. I felt a dart of horror. I shook my head vehemently. 'No!' I said.

It didn't register. He took out a tube of gel from his locker and grabbed me by the arm. Roughly, he shoved me over the end of his bottom bunk bed. He pulled my jeans down and, when I tried to resist, he pushed me down hard and held me there. My impulse was to cry out for help, to scream for someone to get me out of here, but I could hear the boisterous party in full swing, with lots of laughter, shrieks and voices, and I knew I wouldn't be heard. Without delay, the sailor pushed himself into me roughly. I felt my body being torn apart and cried out in agony. But he continued unabated, intent only on getting his way, just the same as when Aidan had raped me.

When he was done, he got his T-shirt and wiped himself off. He left me hanging over the bed as he staggered back to the party without a word. I was bleeding again, but this time the blood was a brighter red, which scared me. What had he done to me? In awful pain, I tried to clean up the mess as best I could with the sailor's dirty T-shirt. The familiar feelings of shame and degradation hung over me. I pulled up my pants, fell on the bunk and sobbed my eyes out. Soon, Danny appeared at my side and stood over me. 'You all right?' He was quite drunk himself, and swaying.

'I've been fucked,' I cried out. I showed him the bloody, wet T-shirt.

'Oh, when you've done it enough, you'll stop bleeding,' he said tersely. 'Anyway, he used gel, didn't he?'

I looked up at Danny in disbelief. He knew I would be raped. He'd set me up for it, the bastard. I hated him with a vengeance at that moment.

'Listen,' Danny continued, slurring his words, 'I've been fucked, what, fifty, a hundred times, altogether. I fuckin' bled every time. My arse wasn't able to take a cock in it either . . . you just get used to it.'

I turned and lay face down, too angry to speak to him.

'Come on, John. Have another drink.' A vodka bottle appeared by my ear. I didn't move. Suddenly, I was pulled up to sitting position, and Danny was beside me on the bunk. He put his arm round me, pulled my head back and threw vodka down my throat. I choked, then swallowed. Then I snatched the bottle out of his hand and glugged. I didn't care any more, about anything or anyone. If they wanted me to do it, I'd do it. Who gave a flying fuck?

'That's my boy,' slurred Danny and slapped me on the back. He steered me back into the party, led me to another sailor and ordered me to give him oral sex. By now, sex was going on all over the mess room and sleeping quarters. There were about eight of us prostitutes altogether and we were being used up to the hilt, as it were.

After the job, I vomited. And, all the time I was doing this job, and then the next two, I held together the cheeks of my bottom, terrified of blood and gunk leaking out. I drank more and more vodka. The 'party' went on until after 3 a.m. I have no memory of how we got home that night.

Next day, I didn't get up for school. I lay in bed feeling battered, bruised and utterly world-weary. I stayed there as long as I could, then got up and went into the back garden. There was a large tree at the end of our garden, and I remember just standing there and staring at it for the longest time. If only I had a rope. I was devoid of all feeling, my head throbbing, my backside aching. My soul had been stolen.

I needed to talk to someone desperately about the terrible trap I was in, but I had no one to turn to, no one I could trust. I returned indoors and spent the remainder of the day there, knowing that night was coming rapidly upon me.

The guys slept all day – why would they get up? They didn't have to work or worry about money: they earned their living from trading my flesh. Eventually, when they did arise, we ate supper in awkward silence. I was sulking with Danny, but he was his usual cheerful self. Neither of them pretended to care. My mother was out. Bernard was at mass, as was his daily routine. And two strangers had taken over my house, and my body, mind and soul.

That night, we went back down the docks, and back to the ships. Danny explained that while the ship was there, the money was there, and we should take it. I had been paid twenty pounds for my troubles – God knows how much the guys had earned from me that first night. The same performance was repeated for another three or four days, until the ship left the dock.

I recall one of the nights walking past an abattoir nearby and hearing the screeches of the scared and trapped cows and pigs. I recognised their fear. I felt like an animal being led to the abattoir, daily, but I was so dead and cold inside that I didn't even know if I could screech anymore. I was stripped of all human feeling.

By the age of twelve and a half, the Dubliners were plotting for ways to make more money from me, before I became too difficult to manage. Nothing ever stays the same, and a power struggle was beginning to take place. I was beginning to fight back occasionally, swearing at them or, at times, refusing a job, and they didn't like it. Sometimes Diarmuid threatened more kidney-bashing violence, and that usually worked to get me back in line. But they didn't want to spoil my looks, so if they did beat me, Diarmuid would make sure I had bruises where the sun didn't shine. Danny would threaten to withhold the meagre amount of money he gave me – which hurt more than punches.

One evening, we were heading to The Penthouse, as usual, when Danny asked, 'Fancy something different tonight?'

'What?' I was grumpy as hell.

'Let's have a drink first, then,' wheedled Danny, knowing how to warm me up.

That night, we had the usual few rounds of drinks before bundling into a taxi, an unknown luxury. Eventually, our cab drew up at a large country house, which ran alongside a small lane. It looked neat and tidy, with a sprawling garden, drystone walls and a fancy iron gate. We tumbled out of the taxi and Danny paid the driver. All three of us started up the garden path. Danny turned to me and said in his most charming voice, 'OK, time to look your sexiest, John. Prepare to smile – it's party time.'

16

House of Horrors

No sooner was I in the front door than I was handed a large scotch in an expensive cut-glass tumbler. Danny led me into a large, dimly lit living room, where there must have been at least fifty men gathered, of all ages, all sizing each other up. They had the look of guys I'd seen at the urinals: furtive, lusty and staring at each other with that hard glare.

Everyone was drinking. There were corks popping, bottles of wine, vodka, scotch and sherry flowing. Beer bottles were being passed around as if the men were on a desert island, dying of thirst. There were also boys amongst the mêlée – rent boys, like me, I assumed.

As the men passed each other, or passed a boy, they put out their hands and touched. There was a lot of touching, groping and kissing going on, and the party had hardly begun. Then the host, a small sweaty man in a suit, with a bald head and spectacles, came up to Danny and whispered in his ear. He was a wealthy gay lawyer, apparently, a well-respected face in the law courts.

He had a rent boy on hand, a slim, tall teenager with bleached blond hair, who wafted past in tight white trousers, similar to mine, wearing only a pink pinny on top. He was handing out tall glasses of pink champagne and wore lots of sparkly eye shadow. As he brushed past, the flushed-looking lawyer smacked his bottom, and they both giggled suggestively.

At a glance, the room was lavish and flamboyant, with leather sofas, crystal lamps and chandeliers, crammed bookcases and exotic rugs and furnishings. There were enormous paintings on the walls and long red velvet curtains at the French doors leading out to what I assumed was the garden. I had never been inside a house of such grandeur in my life before.

There wasn't a woman in sight. In the centre of the room, several boys congregated. They were just like me: dressed in camp clothes, nervous-looking, desperately trying to be cool. We made eye contact but said nothing to each other. Music blasted out of big speakers, giving the place a party atmosphere.

I didn't know exactly what was expected of me, although I could take a good guess. I took cold comfort in the fact that the environment was at least warm and less bleak than a filthy toilet cubicle or the back of a clapped-out car. I was handed a drink, which was quickly replenished with the free-flowing whiskey. As usual, the drink took the edges off my apprehension.

Most of the men in the room were middle-aged and prosperous-looking business types. I also recognised some 'celebrity' faces I'd seen in newspapers, or even TV. I also saw a priest I knew by sight across the room, which surprised but didn't shock me, after the numerous encounters I'd had with the other priest in the docks' toilets. This priest wasn't wearing his collar now and just looked like another mid-life, balding, stocky man, out for a sexual thrill with a child.

This was the mid-seventies and, remarkable as it seems today, homosexuality was still illegal in Ireland. This party was clearly one of the few ways many gay men could come and have sex with each other in the privacy of someone's home. The paedophiles, who weren't necessarily gay, were probably 'happily' married men or single loners, who came to buy and then consume the boys being displayed by their pimps.

By now, I had been performing sexual acts on men for almost five years, the past two under the control of the Dubliners. I realised, standing there, flicking my hair, holding out my 'pinky' finger, sipping my drink and making eye contact with men, that I had mastered the rules of the 'pickup' game. I knew how to turn men on, how to make myself alluring, how to turn away and then look back over my shoulder and flutter my eyelashes and how to display my bottom to its best advantage.

I drank my drink and my glass was refilled yet again. As the lawyer's rent boy passed by, he bent down and whispered to me, 'I see I'm not the only chicken around here this evening.' Then he smiled at me, conspiratorially. I felt included. Perhaps this was my world now. Perhaps this was where I truly belonged.

A guy approached Danny and leaned towards him for a moment. He was young and attractive, different from the others. Danny nodded and smiled over at me. The guy came towards me, grabbed my hand gently and gestured we go upstairs. I looked at Danny, who nodded and gestured 'blow job'. I felt quite drunk by now, and my head was swimming as we ascended the staircase. All around us men were touching each other, kissing and groping, and the living room had a pulsating atmosphere, as if it was going to explode any time soon into a massive orgy.

I was not used to being in a bedroom for sex, and for some reason I felt safer than usual in this domestic setting. Maybe this wouldn't be so bad after all. The guy started to touch me all over to turn himself on – something I had become accustomed to – and he quickly became aroused. He indicated for me to sit on the bed, and I started to perform oral sex. Given his state of arousal, I comforted myself with the thought that it would be over soon. However, it wasn't to be so straightforward. Suddenly, he moved away and went round behind me. Despite my protests, he produced a small tin of Vaseline and began to smear it onto his penis.

I quickly made to escape, but he grabbed me and forced me round again. Pinning me to the bed, all veneer of niceness and civility well gone, he proceeded to rape me. During the gruesome act, I became aware that another man had entered the room. He watched us for a minute, then unzipped his trousers and took out his penis. He was a hefty, important-looking middle-aged man in his fifties, and he came up to where my head was hanging over the bedside and forced his penis into my mouth. A third man appeared and watched the whole scenario for a moment. He then approached me on the other side, unzipped himself, pulled back my right arm and made me masturbate him. I was gagging and in extreme pain as these men grunted and moaned, lost in their own pleasure. I was just a piece of meat with holes in it, a receptacle for the sperm of these three animals.

The minutes passed, slowly, painfully, and my drunken haze fell away. Finally, one by one, they finished themselves off and left me there, collapsed on the bed in a heap, feeling sick as a dog. I was by now completely naked. I listened, as if from a far distance, as the three men headed off together, laughing and chatting, leaving me to clean myself up as best I could. I got up slowly from the bed and dressed myself. I washed out my mouth with whiskey.

On automatic pilot, I went back downstairs, worried, as ever, about the mess that might emerge from my behind. As usual, I communicated my anger to Danny in the only way I knew how: by sulking.

'All right?' he whispered, sidling up to me, drink in hand.

'No, the bastard fucked me.'

'Here's a drink and a ciggie,' came his reply.

I refused to take them, so he thrust them at me, annoyed with me for being difficult. 'Go on, be a good boy – and don't look so fuckin' miserable, it's a party for fuck's sake.'

A drink and a ciggie was the answer to everything, and I learned, very early on, that that was going to be the way to endure whatever life and the Dubliners threw at me. I gulped down my drink in one and had several cigarettes in a row, followed swiftly by more drink.

After that, I was taken into the garden by a drunken, flushed businessman, pushed over a metal garden seat in the chill of the night and penetrated greedily again. By now, I didn't have it in me to care what was happening to me – I was an empty shell.

The priest then made me give him oral sex and used such force that I thought I was going to suffocate. I prayed that he would go straight to Hell, where he belonged. I hoped the hypocrite would burn painfully and slowly. When the job was done, I threw up on the carpet and, in fruitless protest at what was happening me, I didn't bother to clear it up.

The night went on and on, with hand jobs, blow jobs and full penetration, and I eventually lost count of the things that were done to my young body. I drank and drank until oblivion hit me like a club over the head. Again, I have no recollection of getting home, but the next day I felt like death, sick to my stomach from the booze and the abuse. I found twenty-five pounds stuffed into my jeans pocket, my meagre reward for a night of utter degradation. God knows what the Dubliners made from my flesh that night, it must have run into hundreds.

I lay in bed for a long time, wondering how I could go on. Plagued by suicidal thoughts, I once again contemplated methods to take my life. I could take some pills, throw myself off a bridge or hang myself. Anything to make the pain go away, to make everything quiet and peaceful. Compared to the children I saw around me, laughing, shouting and playing football, I felt like I was an alien.

These days, I mitched from school regularly. Warnings from the school made no difference. And, when I did attend, I was often belligerent and out of hand. I was spoiling for a fight with anyone who came my way.

Ironically, I was also still an altar boy – in theory – but the priests I had encountered killed off any religious faith or trust. What a load of claptrap it all was: they were telling us how to live a moral life one minute and hiring young boys as 'chicken' the next. Suffer the little children, Jesus said. They suffered all right, but it would take quite a few more years before that particular pillar of the temple was toppled.

But I was afraid to give up serving mass, not knowing what excuse I could offer to my mother or the local priests. At one point, I even attempted to set up an 'altar boys' union', much to my local priest's horror. Needless to say, and perhaps understandably, the altar boys' union was firmly scotched.

By the time I was an adolescent, I was street wise beyond my years and had experienced a side of life that most people never dreamed existed. I also had a clear understanding of hypocrisy. I practised it on my punters and they, in turn, practised it on their unsuspecting wives and families. We lived in the shadow of statues, were dominated by a cross and were educated to believe in the values of Christian teachings: kindness, charity, do unto others as you would have them do unto you. Such powerful words. How on earth had they become so distorted in my life?

I wondered at all these so-called respectable model citizens, these men, the middle and upper classes who ran Limerick, that I had met at that first house party. They were pillars of the community, just like the very first garda who abused me. Why did they think they had the right to tell us what to do, seemingly upholding the law, while abusing children in their spare time? It filled me with rage, all the more because I was so powerless to do anything about it.

That is, until things suddenly changed, without any warning at all.

The Dubliners' bags were packed when I came home from school. A few weeks had passed since the lawyer's party, and down by the docks it was business as usual. Yet, Danny and

Diarmuid were standing in our living room, ready to head back to Dublin.

'We'll be off then.' Danny sounded like someone who had dropped in for a short visit to a vague acquaintance. 'If you're ever in Dublin, give us a call.'

Diarmuid, as usual, said nothing. Both seemed anxious to make a quick getaway. I was stunned. 'But why are you going? What's wrong?' I asked.

They exchanged a look. Obviously something was up, but they weren't going to tell me about it. 'It's just time to move on,' said Danny. Diarmuid nodded in agreement.

I knew Danny well enough by now to know when he wasn't telling me the truth, which was most of the time. I figured they'd got themselves into hot water with someone over money, or a drugs deal, and they were being threatened. Living on the edge, as they did, it was easy to make enemies and, if drugs were involved, the punishment for an unpaid debt could be swift and brutal. But, no matter how much I questioned them, they weren't prepared to explain why, having lived and worked with me for nearly three years, they were abandoning me at a moment's notice.

They were leaving without saying goodbye to my mother, who wasn't yet home from work. I wondered if they had fallen out with her. Perhaps they owed her rent, which they had been paying up to now out of the money I had earned for them. I suspected they were doing a runner. And not for the first time, I imagined.

'If you're ever up in the big smoke, you'll find us in Rice's Bar or Bartley Dunne's,' said Danny. 'And we'll give you a call, when we get there.'

I watched them disappear down the road and out of sight. I went back inside and sat in the living room. It was only a short while since we'd been to the lawyer's party. The events of the night were still fresh in my mind. I should have felt relieved to see the back of those two bastards, yet my mind was full of mixed emotions. I felt dumped and alone. They had initiated me into their corrupt world, and their habits were now my habits. They'd taught me to drink and smoke hash, to turn tricks, to dress, to do all sorts of extraordinary things. They had been my managers, my family, my everything, since the day of their arrival. In a perverse kind of way, they had adopted me, and I had let them. The life they had shown me was now all I knew.

I figured I was somehow to blame. I'd got older and started to fight back. I had certainly shown them how upset I was after the house party. Maybe they felt I was getting too hard to handle and would spill the beans. Maybe they were off to train up another young boy to take my place. A love–hate relationship can be the most confusing one of all, and my emotions towards those two men veered dangerously from one extreme to the other. I had lived in fear of losing Danny's approval and getting Diarmuid's boot in my back again. But, like a prisoner who had yearned for freedom for years, when the prison gates were finally flung wide open, I was also terrified.

How big and scary the Limerick landscape seemed now that I was alone. Would I be able to manage without them? In my mind, they had been both my gaolers and my protectors. My thoughts turned once again to Aidan, to the grotty sheepskin rug and the flash of cameras. I imagined a fifty pence piece being flung at me when I was used to real money and a certain status as a good-looking rent boy, desired and sought after by my 'clients'. If Aidan and his seedy friends got wind that the coast was clear and came back into my life, that would be the last straw.

I also had to cope with serious addictive habits. I had been drinking a vast amount of spirits on a daily basis for almost three years. I needed drink in the same way as I needed my cigarettes, in the early years, when I was trying to cope with Aidan's abuse. I had also smoked a lot of hash and liked the laid-back feeling it gave me. The question was: how was I going to keep up the habits I had acquired? During my time with the Dubliners, I had got used to having my own money to spend whenever I wanted. I had even managed to save almost one hundred pounds.

These thoughts plagued me as I tried to adjust to the new situation at home. Whatever buffer the Dubliners had provided between me and my mother was now gone. Now there was just the three of us again and, by now, I was estranged from both her and my brother. I went through the motions of living in the family home but, inside, I was numb. I wanted to die.

I'd lived with the idea of death since I was eight years old. At first, it had been a vague notion in which I imagined a white coffin and a weeping family around my graveside. These images had become less romantic as time wore on. I now understood that death could be achieved in many ways. I'd felt dangerously close to it on occasions, especially the night I was almost run over by one of the punters. I was attuned to violence. It went hand in hand with alcohol and lay lightly below the surface of some of the men, whether they frequented the toilets or the posh house. Paedophilia, I had discovered, is a classless crime.

But death by my own hand was different. Suicide gave me a choice, however harsh. A rope, pills, the river, a razor blade. I fantasised how it could be done, quickly and painlessly.

Drinking the whiskey was easy. After the first few shots, I popped the pills into my mouth. By then, I'd lost all sense of danger. I'd searched the house for whatever tablets I could find, paracetamol and sleeping tablets, a cocktail mixed with more whiskey. I imagined my body sinking into a black velvet space. Mostly, I wanted my mind to be still, the voices silent. Was I seriously trying to kill myself? Is it possible to understand what goes on in the deepest level of one's mind? While I willed death to come quickly, my one conscious act was to leave the empty pill bottles on the chest of drawers. I was seriously dicing with death, and I don't recall wanting to be saved on time, but the empty pill bottles were obviously the last bitter cry for help I was sending out. When I finished half a bottle of whiskey and washed down the rest of the pills, I fell onto my bed and swirled into unconsciousness.

Twenty-four hours later, I opened my eyes. My head was pounding, my mouth and eyes dry. A dazed glance around my familiar, untidy room convinced me that I was not in heaven. My mouth was so dry I could hardly swallow, and my heart was racing. I had the shakes and felt sick to the pit of my stomach. I made it to the bathroom just in time and was violently ill. On my way, I caught a glimpse of the pill bottles. They were untouched.

Over the next few days, I recovered. My grand gesture turned out to be nothing more dramatic than a severe bout of vomiting and a pounding headache. Not that I had known that going into it. But now, in its aftermath, I felt a sense of relief that I was still alive. Maybe there was something left to live for, something I had yet to discover.

In the days that followed, as I adjusted to a new routine in the absence of the Dubliners, I also began to feel relief that they were gone from my life. I didn't have to go anywhere or do anything. I was free at last. And I was bigger than before, when I had been only eleven and totally defenceless against Aidan and his lot. Almost three years had passed. I could and would look after myself from now on.

Now that I was no longer out at night, I tried to attend school more regularly. But I was failing badly, well behind the rest of the class. My good intentions didn't last long. I had missed so much, and it all seemed pointless. Secrecy and furtiveness had become my way of life, and I felt marked out as different to the other pupils.

My behaviour in general was becoming more erratic and out of control. The absence of the numbing substances I had become accustomed to over three years being pimped around the docks – drinking and smoking hash – was taking its toll. It occurred to me: what if I turned tricks on my own? For starters, I could keep all the cash for myself. But it was a scary prospect. As much as I had come to resent Danny and Diarmuid conning me out of money, I also valued the protection they provided. That was how I saw it then, at least. In time, I would come to realise how bogus this notion of protection was, the age-old, tried-and-tested foil of the pimp.

I wasn't sure that I could go it alone. However, after a couple of weeks with my money supply dwindling fast, I decided I would continue in the lifestyle to which I had become accustomed. From the age of eight, men had taken their pleasure from me. I was now a fourteen-year-old teenager, skilled at seduction. Knowing how to attract and turn men on seemed the 'natural' thing to do. Sex with men represented a world where I was wanted, prized even, however twisted the nature of the desire. Nowhere else in the world was this reflected back at me.

Within a few weeks of the Dubliners leaving, I found myself heading back down to the docks. It was scary going there alone. I popped in for a drink at our regular dockside pub and met a couple of the women I'd been with on the ship. We got to chatting about our work, and they gave me tips as to how I should operate on my own. At the docks' toilets, I also met people I recognised. Some of the boys and the pimps nodded to me. Word had got out that the lads had gone back to Dublin, and a few of the pimps were eager to 'employ' a freshly available piece of 'chicken'. I turned down these offers and managed by myself to entice a couple of punters.

While I was hanging around the toilets, I started talking to a man, we'll call him Bert Sylvester. He was older than me and told me he had also been a rent boy for years. This was reassuring. He looked fit and healthy, a survivor. He was gay and just came down for some casual sex, or sometimes to make some money. He was very theatrical, a real wit, and we hit it off immediately. Afterwards, we went for a drink and discovered we had some mutual acquaintances, including the lawyer whose party I had attended.

Soon we were heading back there together, to another party. Over the next few months, we attended about five altogether. Working alone now, there were risks and dangers, and I experienced things I'd never experienced when the Dubliners were around.

Prostitution can only exist on double standards and blind eyes being turned. It wasn't only pimps who were a threat. Danny had told me it could happen. One of the women prostitutes had verified it. Both had personal experiences of the powerful arm of the law. I, too, knew what could happen when a garda asked me to give him a hand. Garda McEvoy had left his mark on my young mind, but I was older now, tough, a man of the world, or so I liked to believe.

When I saw the squad car cruising by the toilets I wasn't that bothered. This happened from time to time. Danny had told me the guards knew all about what went on and turned a blind eye to it most of the time. Apparently, on occasion, they'd swoop down and sweep people up to teach them a lesson, but in the three years I'd been working my nightly routine, I'd never been bothered by the police. However, this night – about a month after the guys had disappeared back to Dublin – I became aware that this garda patrol car was continuing to cruise back and forth, around the bridge. A guard peered out the window at me. I shuffled back into the shadowy doorway to hide, but it was too late.

A minute later, he appeared in front of me. He grabbed my shoulder and pushed me hard up against the wall.

'What are you doing here, boy?'

'Nothin'.'

'I'll give you nothin'.' With that, he dragged me off by the arm and pushed me into the back of his patrol car. At the garda station, I was hauled from the car and into the police station. 'You're out of control, young man,' he snapped.

Next, I was dragged down a grey, low-lit corridor and,

still struggling, was flung into a cell. 'Get in there, you scum,' he shouted. He banged shut the steel door, then flicked open the slit in it to check on me.

I'd never been in a cell before and was terrified at the thought of what would happen if he brought my mother down there. I imagined her wrath. I was in a panic. I remember repeating over and over in my head, 'Everyone's going to kill me . . .'

After a few minutes, I lay down on the thin, stinking foam mattress and tried to calm myself down. As I regained some composure, I began to feel a strange sense of relief. Everything could come out now. My double life would finally be exposed. My mother would know what I was doing, as would the police, my family, friends, neighbours and school. I'd be all over the papers and, no doubt, I'd be sent to a borstal, to be reformed. The idea of being put into care or a juvenile home suddenly didn't seem so bad. Maybe it was a good thing that the game was up, at last.

A key turned in the lock. The guard who had thrown me into the cell opened the door. I sat up on the bed, wondering what was going to happen next. Was I going to have to fill out a statement? Would I be arrested? Would I have a lawyer? Was my mother already at the station? The guard hovered in the doorway a moment. He was a stocky, middle-aged man, still in his long, dark overcoat with its shiny silver buttons.

'I know what you were doing down there,' he barked menacingly. 'I know what you young fellas get up to down the

Dock Road. It's disgusting.' He looked at me like I was a piece of dirt. I imagined that was how everyone would look at me once they found out what I was doing. I'd felt it often enough myself.

He clanged the door shut behind him and strode into the cell and over to where I sat. I decided to keep as still as I could and not say anything. He opened his coat and then his fly. His pot belly hung over his uniform trousers. 'If you say a fuckin' word about this, I will cut your throat, so help me,' he said through gritted teeth.

Before I could move, he grabbed me by the hair, pulled me forward on the bed and pushed his penis into my mouth. His coat provided a screen to anyone who happened to look through the slit in the door. When he came, he grabbed my hair and held it, so I couldn't get away.

I retched and violently threw up all over the floor. I wiped my mouth on my sleeve as he calmly put his penis back into his trousers and zipped up. I stared at him with pure hatred. He didn't return my gaze.

He then dragged me to my feet, opened the door and hauled me back outside and into the squad car. I assumed he was going to drive me home to confront my mother. However, he returned to the spot where he had picked me up, outside the toilet door. Job done. I realised well enough by now what his game was. He was cruising himself, and I was a freebie. Far safer to conduct business in the privacy of a police cell. This wouldn't be the last time I'd see him, either.

That night, I stumbled the long way home, in the pitch dark, sick to the stomach. I felt at the lowest ebb ever and resolved to get the hell out of Limerick as soon as I possibly could.

17

On the Run

It was around this time, after the horrific incident in the garda station, that I began to run away on a regular basis. Sometimes I hitched to Dublin or Cork; sometimes I jumped onto the back of a lorry and had a free ride. These episodes were usually triggered by some violent incident or trouble in school or at home. Sometimes I sneaked onto trains and persuaded the ticket collector that my mother was further up the train. Or I'd hide in the toilets, avoiding the ticket collector altogether. On one occasion, I rode all the way to Rosslare, lying in the back of an open truck among the goods. I was possessed of a dangerous recklessness, beyond fear of authority or even death. When I arrived at my destination, I would sleep in burnt-out cars, or in cardboard boxes, under bridges or in the doorways of shops and churches. I felt as safe there as anywhere.

But I had the instincts of a homing pigeon and always ended up making my way back to Limerick where things picked up again exactly where they left off, as if nothing had happened. I was in free fall. Although, in the main, I maintained the daytime farce of going through the motions at school, along with my night-time routine, inside I was falling apart.

I wanted to lash out at the world, but most of my destructive tendencies were turned inwards. One time, I persuaded a friend of mine, George, who was one of the wild boys at school, to draw out his savings – a substantial seventy pounds – and take the train with me to Dublin. We'd been friends when we were children, kicking ball around the street, and, although our lives had gone in different directions, we still got on well together. We travelled in style and even got as far as Dublin airport, where we became very drunk after ordering double Bacardis and cokes at the airport bar. Seventy pounds had seemed like a fortune when we began our journey, but it was soon whittled away. One of my sisters lived in Dublin. I knew she had a long back garden, and I decided that that was where we would camp.

Once we had slept off the drink, we hung out there for a few days, unnoticed. My sister was in hospital with a complicated pregnancy, and her husband had more important matters on his mind than checking out the end of his garden. We kept warm by burning some tinder we found and slept under the stars. We had nothing to cover us but the clothes we were wearing, and the nights were cold, particularly when I awoke in the small hours and wondered what the hell we were doing. To survive, we stole milk from doorsteps or bread from shop doorways. We even rummaged through dustbins and sometimes begged for money from passers-by.

Eventually, we heard someone coming up the steps from the neighbouring garden, and we jumped over the wall into another back garden to hide. The people in that house saw us and called the gardaí, who came and caught us. We were scolded and then handed over to my brother-in-law who was furious with us. I remember a piece of advice he gave me. 'If you don't amount to anything by the time you're thirty-five, you will never be anything.'

I was a teenager and wired to the moon. Thirty-five was ancient and, at the rate I was living, the idea of lasting another twenty years was inconceivable. But his words stayed in my mind and would come back to spur me on when, in my twenties, I struggled to get my life together again.

George's mother arrived on the train to fetch us. She had been frantically worried about her son and he received a strict warning to stay away from me. I was a bad influence. I couldn't disagree with her opinion but, in my own home, when I finally turned up on the doorstep looking the worse for wear, no questions were asked as to the whys and wherefores of any disappearance.

I was soon back to my wild ways and ended up drinking poitín with another boy I knew. This home-brewed Irish spirit, I'd heard, was renowned for rotting the brain and could even make you go blind. So what, I thought, knocking it back. I'd seen enough to last me a lifetime. I was also offered cocaine but didn't take it. I don't know why exactly. Perhaps, at some gut survival level, I knew that if I did, I would be completely lost. I had seen people zoned out on drugs in the toilets and pubs. Once I went down that path, I might never come back. Hash was as far as it went. This one point of self-awareness in my early teens probably saved my life later on. I already sensed I was in trouble with alcohol. I had no idea, however, of just how bad it would get. I couldn't go for a day without it. I didn't recognise it at the time but, by the time I was in my mid-teens, I had slipped into alcoholism. Then, two things happened to interrupt the awful routine of my life. The first was very sad, the second, hugely exciting.

When I was a child, I used to visit my Uncle Jimmy in his small overcrowded shoeshop. Shoes were piled high, and the smell of rubber and polish filled the air.

As I grew older, he'd get me to deliver the bags of newly heeled shoes. He was a big, kindly man with rough, working hands. 'There'll be a few bob for your trouble,' he'd say.

I'd grab the parcels and run like the wind, delivering them as fast as I could. Uncle Jim would have disappeared into the pub over the road to down a few pints, while I ran the errands. I'd rush back up to the pub for my reward, which I would duly spend on cigarettes.

When, around this time, Uncle Jimmy died, I felt a keen sense of loss. I held him in high esteem, despite not having seen him much in recent years. During his wake – the old Irish custom where people come to the house to pay their respects to the dead – I met a girl who, for obvious reasons, I will call Sarah.

We got to talking and, later, while the adults were still waking Uncle Jim, we ended up back at my own house, in my bedroom. I was streetwise yet clueless about women, and Sarah was a high-spirited young woman who knew exactly what she wanted.

'Have you ever been with a girl before?' she asked.

'Many times,' I lied to her as we lay on the bed.

Although I had never been aroused by any of the sexual acts I'd performed, I had wondered many times if I was gay. I saw boys and girls my own age walking through the town with their arms around each other. It seemed natural, easy, exciting. Apart from a few awkward kisses I'd exchanged with a couple of girls, I had never had a girlfriend and had a very skewed idea of what constituted a relationship. I had no idea of what love, trust, mutual care or respect were really about. My father had died so young, and I had never seen my mother relating to anybody properly in a loving partnership. To me, 'relating' was all about either being bullied or being bought.

But this was different. Our kisses were exploratory, and I soon discovered the answer to my question. I was most definitely, and in the most obvious way possible, a full-blooded, and, by now, fully aroused heterosexual male.

However, I was unsure how I should proceed. Sarah looked bemused when it was obvious I had no idea where my penis was supposed to go. Not knowing there was any other way to make love to a woman, I tried to insert it between her closed legs. I kept assuring her that I'd done it this way before with many girls and it had worked. Only later would I see the irony in a situation where I, with all my expertise, was as clueless as any shy virgin blustering and fumbling his way through his first experience.

Luckily, Sarah took control and gently guided me into her. But it was no good. I was out of my depth . Finally, I came clean with her and told her it was my first time. She was nice about it, and we decided to leave it for the time being.

A couple of weeks later, we tried again. By that time, I'd had a chat with a couple of older guys I knew. This time, I succeeded in losing my virginity. That was how I saw it. The other times, the excruciating, brutal attacks, were nothing to me. With this new discovery that sex could be a mutual pleasure, with a caring aftermath, I believed I could wipe out what had gone before. Sarah and I both knew we weren't in love but, while it lasted, it was good. I will always remember it as the first proper sexual experience I'd had that wasn't tinged with associations of shame and self-loathing.

I know that I appeared wild and uncontrollable to most people, and probably to Sarah too. Emotionally, I was all over the place. I had no idea who I was, or what I wanted to be. The pattern of looking for somewhere to belong, or someone to latch on to, who could give me affection and love, was well and truly established.

Despite my first venture into the heterosexual world, where I knew I belonged, I continued to attend the house parties in the lawyer's house. The glamorous setting was in stark contrast to the foul-smelling toilets where much of my activity took place. Not that it made much difference. Although this man lived his life in an open way, he still had the same furtive tendencies and would demand my services while his live-in boyfriend was otherwise engaged.

At one such party, I met a man who would, in time, come to represent in my mind the father I'd always wanted. He was suave and good-looking, a successful businessman from Dublin. Over the course of the night, he talked to me in a way that no one else ever had before. He told me I was too good to be working down the docks. I deserved better from life. He had a charismatic personality and I hung on to his every word, knowing he spoke the truth. Despite going solo after the Dubliners left, and behind my new-found bravado, I knew the risks. I had been raped again on a number of occasions by punters, especially when I'd had too much to drink.

This man told me I was worth something. I tried extra hard to please him sexually and it was obvious from the attention he continued to pay me that he was attracted to me. Usually, I faked affection for these men during our brief encounters but, on this occasion, I was aware of a definite bond being forged between us. It was obvious that he was popular with the guests, and he moved at his ease among them. I admired his clothes and his confident manner and wanted, more than anything, to be like him. I wondered if he would provide me with a way out of Limerick, an escape route from my messed-up life.

If I could just be with one person who cared, then, I believed, all my problems would be solved. He too was of the same opinion. Before the night was over, he told me he wanted to be my friend and have a special relationship with me. He told me he loved me. He had uttered the words I had waited a lifetime to hear.

When it was time to part, he gave me his card and said, 'If you get fed up of it here, ring me, and I will make sure there's a train ticket to Dublin ready for you.'

I could not believe my ears. This time I could run away, and there would be someone at the end of the journey to take care of me. For a short while after that meeting, I continued working the usual routine and attending school on and off. I couldn't get him out of my head. I rang his office. I was prepared to be disappointed. But he was as good as his word. A train ticket was organised. Without a word to anyone, I mitched off school, packed a few things into a rucksack, grabbed whatever money I had left and headed for the train to Dublin.

I looked at the fields and houses as they flashed past and imagined life in the capital city. I could start again, free at last. Life was starting afresh, all thanks to Shea, as we'll call him, my new friend. He greeted me with the same warmth he had shown at the party and, over the following weeks, what unfolded was like a scene out of a gay *Pygmalion*.

He was my new 'mentor'. He wanted to smooth away my rough edges and I was only too willing to follow his advice. He bought me new clothes, taught me the correct way to use a knife and fork, how to speak and behave, and how to drink fine wine. I was a sponge, eager to soak up everything he told me. He said he loved me, and I believed I was falling in love with him. Nobody had ever shown me such care or concern. I became a frequent drinker in Bartley Dunne's where the Dubliners told me they hung out. I looked out for them but, thankfully, I never met them there. I was content with my new life and did not want any complicated reminders of the old days.

In the gay bars in Dublin, I saw the usual variety of types, including those who were closet gays, many of them married men. Then there were the loners. I suspected that some of these were paedophiles of the Aidan variety and stayed as far away as I could from them.

Shea liked to be accompanied by a good-looking teenager and I was his chosen one. I gave him sex whenever he wanted it and would also oblige some of his friends when he suggested it. Sex of this kind was commonplace and meant nothing to me. I told myself I was secure in my new relationship with him. I understood how the gay scene worked and had no desire to seek the same pleasure for myself from Shea. Not that I would have obtained it. Reciprocation was not part of our deal, and that was fine by me. I would do anything to please him and trusted him implicitly.

During my time in Dublin with Shea, I was also introduced to the city's equivalent of the Limerick 'parties' that had been held in the lawyer's house. They were just as bad as the worst of the Limerick ones, held in the residences of a wealthy circle who enjoyed sex with boys. I was expected, as ever, to 'service' those who desired it. By this stage, however, there was little that could shock me.

Here, I mixed with the upper echelons of society, men of wealth from across the professional classes – men who stood to lose a lot should their secret proclivities ever be exposed. But they didn't look like they were too worried: they felt impervious to the constraints of the real world, its concerns below them. And, as well as being above the law, as they saw it, they were tight-knit. To get into this circle, no doubt, one would have to prove himself worthy, and a safe bet. Not so for the rent-boys, though: we were just fodder, seen in no way as a threat. If we opened our mouths to speak, who would believe us anyway?

After two weeks of my new life, Shea suggested I return home and continue my education. A good education was essential, he insisted, if I was to make anything of myself. I was in my mid-teens; soon I would be a man, able to make my way in the world. If I did not have that security behind me, I would amount to nothing, especially as I was living such a reckless life.

My brother-in-law had given me the same advice and I had tossed it carelessly aside. Coming from Shea, it carried weight. Reluctantly, I said goodbye to him and promised I would come and visit him again soon.

Back home, I tried to settle down. I kept remembering his words but I was so far behind in class it was impossible to concentrate or make the effort to catch up. All I could think about was returning to Dublin as quickly as possible. Shea and I kept in touch by phone. I'd ring him from public phones, afraid my mother or brother would discover what was going on, and we'd chat briefly before he was called away. He had a busy lifestyle, and I was afraid he would forget me as he went on his usual round of parties and social events. You could say he had given me notions above myself, and it was difficult to settle back to the same old grind. I missed him every day and when I could stand the separation no longer I decided to surprise him with a visit.

I hitched a ride from Limerick. I was a puppy pining for his master and, all the way to Dublin, my excitement grew at the thought of being part of his life again.

When I arrived in the city, I was lost. I'd never gone anywhere without Shea and, although I was used to the fast pace of a large city, this was unfamiliar territory. I knew he lived south of the Liffey, somewhere near the coast. I walked towards the Monkstown area and, to my surprise, after searching around for about an hour, I found his house. I knocked on the door but he was not at home. This didn't surprise me. He was always off somewhere, and my only fear was that he was out of the country on business or holidays.

Clumps of trees grew opposite his house. I settled down to wait for his arrival. If he had not returned by nightfall, I'd find shelter in a shop doorway. Despite the fact that I was in a strange city, I had no fear of sleeping on the streets. It began to rain. With no coat or umbrella, I was getting soaked, but the trees provided some shelter. An hour went by, then another. I continued to wait. I'd brought a couple of beers with me but, when I finished them, I could feel my impatience beginning to get the better of me. In the end, I made a bed from newspapers and leaves and tried to get some sleep. But the rain persisted, seeping into my clothes and into the ground. I needed a bottle of whiskey to keep out the cold, but I had neither the money nor the inclination to find an off-licence. Eventually, exhausted, I fell asleep.

The car lights woke me up. They swept across the darkness as the driver pulled up and parked outside the house. I recognised Shea's Mercedes. I was shivering from the rain and aware that I probably looked a sight. But by that stage I didn't care. I scrambled to my feet, eager to see him. He stepped out of the car and stood for a moment, waiting for a second person to emerge from the passenger seat. I stepped back into the shadows. The car was now in darkness but, under the street lights, I saw a young man, probably about twenty, move around the car and walk towards the house with Shea.

I knew instantly what was going on. The scene was as familiar to me as the back of my hand. It should not have mattered. I had hung around the gay scene long enough to know that sex was a casual encounter, quickly forgotten, and, unless one was in a close relationship, fidelity was not to be expected. But I had expected it. In my naivety, I had believed him when he told me he loved me.

I picked up one of the empty beer bottles and rushed across the street. He turned when he heard me. I brandished the bottle and yelled obscenities. The young man watched this exchange with streetwise eyes and made sure to stay out of my way. Shea remained calm, but his voice hardened as he explained the ways of his world. 'It's the gay scene,' he said. 'It's what happens. Get used to it, John.'

I was beyond caring. I went for him with the bottle. His companion, now behind me, caught my arm before I could inflict any damage. They wrestled the bottle from my hand. It smashed to the ground and, as Shea hurried into his house, accompanied by his new boyfriend, I collapsed against the wall and sobbed helplessly.

Shea came back and helped me to my feet. He felt bad, but he made it clear that the relationship between us was over. I could clean myself up and stay in his house for the night. Tomorrow I was to return to Limerick. His voice brooked no argument. End of story.

I entered the house with him and was directed to the small guest room. The master bedroom would be occupied by his new boyfriend. I lay in the dark and seethed. It was impossible not to hear the sounds from their room. My anger soon gave way to humiliation then despair. I didn't sleep all night.

Next morning, once Shea had left for work, his new companion made coffee. Instead of being annoyed by my behaviour the previous night, he was good-natured about the whole thing. I accepted a mug of coffee from him, and we sat at the kitchen table talking. Like Shea, he repeated the same advice. 'You'll get over this,' he said. 'You have to. It's just the way things happen.'

'Thing is,' I said, near to tears, 'I've actually fallen in love with him.'

'I know,' he replied. 'But you're not gay, this is a passing phase.'

This was news to me. 'What do you mean, I'm not gay?'

'Sure, you're not gay any more than I'm Shirley Bassey,' he said. I managed a smile – he was trying to cheer me up. 'Listen, Shea isn't for you. He does this to everybody, he'll do it to me. I guarantee he'll be with somebody else by tomorrow night.'

'And you don't mind?' I felt shocked at how casual he was about it all.

'It's just the way it is,' he said.

'Fine,' I said, not meaning it.

He was telling me nothing I did not already know. I'd seen the gay scene in action, but I had somehow convinced myself that this was different. Some gay people fell in love and stayed together. Why not us? Shea was the focus of all the pain I had suppressed over the years and dangerous emotions were bubbling close to the surface.

Back in Limerick, I cried bitterly on the shoulder of my friend Bert, one of the few people I could open up to. Bert listened patiently and reiterated the same advice. My heart would be broken over and over again if I went down that path. But I couldn't get over it and suffered the effects of this betrayal in the months that followed.

A few weeks later, night began to fall as I hitched at the edge of the Dublin Road. Once again, I was heading off to Dublin on one of my aimless jaunts. The affair with Shea still hurt. I had only the vaguest hope that he might reconsider and take me back into his life again, although he had done nothing to suggest this was a possibility.

Life in Limerick was the same as always. I was continuing the usual routine of picking up punters and doing what was expected of me. Business was good. Word was out that I was a skilled chicken. I was on a conveyor belt and could turn a trick with the best of them. As a result, I was a regular guest at the lawyer's parties, where I made more contacts. In this environment, I encountered Limerick businessmen and members of the upper echelons. But, despite the relative comfort of the new environment, what I had to perform still revolted me, and the urge to escape my life never left me. Only problem was, I never knew what I was running towards.

On this particular night, I hoped to get to Dublin and maybe, just maybe, I might bump into Shea in one of the pubs I used to frequent with him. If I had a second chance, I would be more mature about the relationship and would accept what he was willing to give me, even if it was just an occasional night of his company. These thoughts were running through my mind when a car drew up alongside me.

A man leaned out of the window. 'Are you the chemist's son?' he asked.

'No, I'm not,' I told him.

'Where are you headed?'

I told him I was visiting a sick aunt in Dublin but did not have enough money for the train fare. I lied with ease, by now it was second nature to me.

'Climb in,' he said, 'it's too late to get to Dublin tonight, but, if you want, I have a spare room, and you can stay the night and start off again tomorrow.'

It seemed like a plan. At least, by morning, I'd have some of the journey covered. It was also a relief not to have to spend the night in the open. The man drove me to his house, in a suburb at the edge of town.

Once inside, he offered me some home brew. By now, I

never said no to a drink. He poured me a glass of red wine and told me his name was Seamus Connery. His clothes were on the flamboyant side and I noticed that he wore an embroidered waistcoat. Looking around his house, which was full of theatrical memorabilia, I realised he was involved in the acting world. I'd met actors at parties but I'd never come across him before. His small house was full of masks, dressing-up clothes, theatre programmes, pictures of him acting. I would later discover he was well known in the thespian world in Limerick. I enjoyed his company and the drink he freely offered. He was clearly an entertainer. I relaxed as he regaled me with funny stories about his times on the stage.

I had several glasses of home-brew wine. It was strong stuff and, when it was time to hit the sack, I was so drunk I could hardly stand. I vaguely remember being put to bed in the spare room, as he'd suggested. Some time later, I woke up. I can't pretend I was surprised, shocked or betrayed to feel his weight on me. On some level, I'd almost expected it. Wherever I went, I met men who just had one thing in mind: using and abusing me.

It was soon apparent that he was masturbating himself as he lay on top of me. He ejaculated over me, then left the room. I was still very drunk and soon fell asleep again. Next morning, he repeated the same scene, telling me he liked 'chicken' and could have 'plenty of chicken' whenever he wanted it.

He didn't give me any money, but he eventually set me out on the road to Dublin. The desire to see Shea had worn off. Hungover and disheartened by this encounter, I turned round and headed back into Limerick.

18

Waiting for the Healer

My behavior at school continued to deteriorate. I constantly gave cheek to the teachers and tried to wind them up. With all respect for authority gone, the words and actions came easily to me. On one such occasion, an elderly male teacher, who obviously couldn't take any more, told me bitterly, 'The wrong fuckin' brother died.' This was a bridge too far and I lost it. I jumped over the desk and hit him in the face.

I was promptly suspended. It was only two weeks before my Intermediate Certificate Exams and, perhaps surprisingly, I used the time to study hard. I passed the exams with flying colours, much to the surprise of my teachers and, more to the point, myself. Perhaps Shea was right. Education mattered.

But I was too far gone to really care. As my behaviour at school continued to deteriorate, it wasn't long before I was expelled, this time for threatening to set the school on fire. By now, I couldn't care less. I hated everything and everyone, the original 'angry young man'. Predictably, Mammy was livid. She called on my middle sister, Deirdre, who lived away from home, to come and reason with me. But it was too little, too late. I was happy to be expelled. All I wanted was to be free: from school, from being controlled, from having to do things I didn't want to do.

Deirdre had no idea about what I had been through in the years since she had left home. She knew nothing of my sordid past or of just how damaged I was. She tried to reason with me, to get me to agree to attend a boarding school, if she could get me into one. She assured me that my sisters, all working now, would each contribute to the cost. But though she tried hard to find a place for me, nowhere would take me. My reputation preceded me; I was too big a risk.

Eventually, I agreed to attend 'The Red Tech', an institution for hard-nosed, tough kids. I would meet my match there. These pupils would break their desks and even strike the teachers. They were afraid of nothing and no one. I knew some whose mothers worked as prostitutes and whose fathers were in jail. They came from rough backgrounds and, like me, were misfits.

Within two weeks of being at the school, the principal Mr Burke, called me into his office. He looked at me hard for a moment. 'You're not getting on here, are you?' he said.

'I don't want to fuckin' get on,' I rudely replied.

He stared at me, thinking hard. 'We teach metalwork here, and you're not interested in learning it at all, are you?'

'Did you not hear what I said first time?'

Mr Burke kept up his hard gaze, looking like he'd had enough of me already. I was told in no uncertain terms to leave the school.

I went home and broke the news to my mother, whose reaction was to be expected. She'd done her best to get me into another school and, once again, I'd thrown away the opportunity. Being 'bad' was the only satisfaction I knew. I no longer made any distinction between positive and negative attention. All that mattered was getting through another day.

I was now fifteen years old. My life was set on a certain course, and there seemed to be no alternative but to follow it to its end, which, at times, offered only two choices, suicide: or death from addiction.

One night, soon after the end of my schooling, I was in the local pub with my mother and some of her friends. I wasn't in the way of much gainful employment those days, a spot of DJing at parties and in pubs and, the odd time, a drag act that I'd created with a friend, which earned us money from local clubs and bars. When we were rehearsing, bouncing jokes and songs off each other, perfecting our lines and collapsing with laughter over our own jokes, it seemed inconceivable that dark suicidal thoughts could haunt me.

But they were never far from my mind, especially in the aftermath of a long drinking session.

Now, it appeared, another avenue of escape was opening up. As the night progressed, one of my mother's friends mentioned a job that was going in a local taxi-cab company. They needed someone to answer the phone. Would I be interested in an interview?

I was already earning money in ways that would have seemed incomprehensible to the assembled gathering. The opportunity to do a job where my hands were clean and my mind at rest at the end of a working day was tempting. I told her I was interested.

The woman passed on my name to the taxi-cab manager and I was soon called for an interview. I got the job and was employed as a night-time base operator, sending out taxis to different destinations. As I controlled the switchboard, checking in with the various drivers, keeping control over the incoming calls, I began to feel a slight stirring of pride in my ability to manage the hectic routine.

But my old way of life continued, though less so now, and I could see no way out of it. Despite being older and street-wise beyond my fifteen years, I was still as lost as ever when it came to freeing myself from the secretive, murky world into which I'd been drawn. On my time off from the taxi company, I was still drinking heavily, still turning tricks.

*

One of the taxi drivers was called Paddy Mullins. He was friendly and kind, the sort of man I would have turned into a father figure in my mind when I was younger. At the end of my night shift, he would come in and talk to me about how the shift had gone and relate some of the crazy incidents that are part and parcel of being a taxi driver. Like Mr Conroy, I had an older man who cared about me in a fatherly way – with no ulterior motive. It was a revelation. In the beginning, it was difficult to accept. But time showed me that I still could have faith in the goodness of people.

Paddy was obviously an intuitive man, and I think he sensed, without me ever having to say it, that my life was out of control. At the end of the shift, he would give me a lift home and he always stopped at a local café, which served a decent burger and chips into the early hours.

We'd sit opposite each other in the café and he'd tell me about his family. He was proud of his children, anxious that they should succeed in life. He sometimes mentioned his teenage son who intended joining the army when he reached seventeen.

I'd eat my burger and chips and listen, enjoying his company but paying little heed to the detail. The army came up in conversation a few times and, occasionally, Paddy would gently suggest that I consider joining. Again, I paid little heed. Marching and drilling did not appeal to me, I'd had enough experience of taking orders.

One night some time later, in the same café, Paddy leaned

across and said, 'I'll be up for you tomorrow, about twelve o'clock, all right?'

'What?' This was new. 'Where are we going?'

'Oh, just out for a drive,' he said casually.

The following midday, when Paddy's rattling old Hillman Hunter taxi drew up at my house and he beeped his horn, I was still in bed. He was early. After a minute or two, the knock came on the door, and I reluctantly got up and got ready.

We set out on our journey, to the barracks, as he revealed to me. When we arrived, he turned to me. 'John, you are going to join the army,' he said, quietly and decisively.

'What?' I looked into his kindly, worn face and realised he was deadly serious. 'You're kidding me.'

I had gone along with him because I had become used to following the course of least resistance. Now, the reality was upon me.

'John, listen to me.' He leaned in and looked straight into my eyes. 'If you don't join the army, you are going to remain a base operator or taxi driver for the rest of your life. Worse still, you'll spend every penny you earn on drink, and you'll end up a bum on the streets. You'll be a nobody, a loser. I don't want to see you end up in gaol. The army will help to give you discipline and a sense of direction in your life.'

I was stunned. I'd heard this advice before from Paddy and knew his son had now joined up. But his son was completely different to me, and his family was a proper, functioning group who did normal things together, like going to the cinema or on holidays, or making family decisions on what was in the best interests of their children.

'No, I won't do it,' I said. I would never fit in there, just like I had never fitted in at home, in school, anywhere.

But Paddy was patient with me. 'Y'know John,' he said quietly, 'sometimes in life we have to take risks. I'm not talking about doing mad, destructive things . . . I'm talking about taking a step forward.'

I looked at Paddy. My God, he really was serious. He wanted me to take myself seriously and stop mucking about. I was being offered a chance. Suddenly, like the taxi-company job, I was being offered an opportunity that was not mired in filth and deceit. I had to make this leap of faith.

'You deserve more,' whispered Paddy, sensing some kind of shift in me.

In reply, I opened the car door and headed down the path towards the recruitment office, with Paddy by my side. When I got there, I discovered that Paddy had phoned ahead to tell them he was bringing in a new recruit. How confident was that? The desk sergeant was friendly and passed me a form to fill in. Within half an hour, it was duly signed and my fate was sealed. I was in the army now. The sergeant told me I would be contacted during the next week to begin my training.

As I walked back towards the car, I walked tall. I felt I had taken a significant step. I got in the passenger seat and Paddy looked at me, happily. 'I did it,' I said. 'I'm in the army.'

Pleased as Punch, Paddy's face broke into an enormous
smile and he shook my hand warmly. 'That's my boy,' he said
and patted me on the back, just like a real father would do.
'You won't regret this, John. This is the beginning of your
new life.'

He was right. I would spend the next three years in the army,
and end up a three-star private. But I'd have a mountain to
climb to get there. Up to that point, my life had been messy
and undisciplined. With my respect for authority long gone
and a past I would not have wished on my worst enemy, I was
suddenly transported to another world. One where discipline
mattered. Where rules had to be obeyed. The willfulness that
had plagued me during my schooldays, my riotous behaviour
and cheekiness, had no place in this new life I had chosen.
But old traits don't die overnight. It was second nature by
now for me to rebel against authority, and I found the
snobbishness of the officer class difficult to endure. This gave
me something to kick against, and to overcome.

I applied to one officer and asked to be allowed sit my
Leaving Certificate examination. He tore up my application
form and demanded to know why a private serving in the
army would want an education. The downside of army life
was its old-fashioned and class-ridden structures.

The routine of early rising and regular mealtimes suited
me. I learned to march in step in more ways than one. I held
my shoulders back and my head high. I liked myself in

uniform. I thought about Thomas Ashe. He had once worn a uniform and had died for a noble cause. I'd often felt close to death. But, if my young life had ended, my cause would have been far from noble. But my old life was behind me. I was no longer a rent-boy. I had an opportunity to learn life skills and practical skills. Most importantly, my sense of self-worth and self-awareness grew enormously. I was seventeen years old and I had a purpose at last.

However, the army could not solve every problem, particularly my alcoholism. One of the most significant and damaging legacies of my troubled childhood was my drinking problem, although it would be a very long time before I would be able to acknowledge it as such. I was well known among my peers as someone with a 'big swallow'. I would drink up to seven pints most nights and, if I hit the spirits, the sky was the limit.

Now, three years after joining the army, I had served my time, and I had to find my way in the world. Apart from my Intermediate Certificate, I lacked a proper education. This was the recession-ridden 1980s' in Ireland, and Limerick was not immune to its effects. Unemployment was high and my prospects of finding a serious job without the necessary qualifications were poor.

I became involved in an endless run of part-time jobs. Naturally, I gravitated towards bar and entertainment work: being a bouncer, DJing, doing my drag act. And most of these jobs brought me into close daily proximity with alcohol, so my boozing continued – and grew – unabated.

What I didn't understand fully at the time was I had a genetic predisposition towards alcoholism. Added to this, the bottle was a coping mechanism, and the only one I knew. My chaotic way of life often meant I was hungover and disorganised. However, I was always functional.

I struggled to decide what to do with myself in the longer term. Despite what I had been brought up to believe, deep down I felt I had something to give. In the army, this sense of myself as an intelligent being had crystallised. I simply needed to find a way forward.

When I first considered becoming a solicitor, I laughed at myself. I remembered the army officer dismissing my Leaving Certificate application form and wondered what he would say if I confided my newly formed ambition to him. I could just imagine. But a tiny seed had formed and was beginning to take root.

My desire to train in law was partly to do with the sense of injustice I felt. I'd seen both sides of society and understood that there was a double standard at work right across the professional classes. Authority figures demanded that we should behave in a certain way, then themselves acted with impunity outside the law. No matter how hard I tried to shake off the rent-boy memories, I kept seeing those young underage boys standing around the walls waiting to be chosen. I wanted to take on the establishment. I wanted to understand a legal system that so often seemed to let down ordinary people, like myself and those around me.

However, I didn't really believe I had a hope in hell of ever achieving my ambition. My past record spoke volumes. Expelled three times from school and a career as a rent-boy was hardly going to look good on my CV. Despite the confidence I'd gained in the army, my self-esteem was low, and I couldn't imagine I would ever get myself into a position where I could earn a decent, legitimate crust, especially in the legal profession.

I have to thank my sister Deirdre for the final kick in the rear that helped me on my way towards struggling out of my chaos. She was living in England, and I travelled over on a brief trip to visit her. One night, when I was very drunk, I started moaning about how I was wasting my life. She endured this self-pitying tirade for as long as she could before pulling me up sharply.

She proceeded to tell me that I was the only one who could help myself. I had intelligence and if I could link that with ambition and willpower, I could make something of myself. We talked until the small hours. I made a drunken vow that I would try to go back to education – which I'd failed to finish – to which Deirdre retorted, 'Yeah, John, seeing is believing.' She was offering me a challenge, and her straight-talking served to sober me up a little and further ignite the spark within me.

*

I returned to Ireland and, straight away, I registered to sit my Leaving Cert. With this qualification in tow, I hoped to get a place in college. I was receiving unemployment benefit and was therefore entitled to some training and government support, without which I could not have done it. A few years had passed since I'd left the army, and returning to school well into my twenties wasn't easy. I was still drinking heavily and doing my usual array of part-time jobs. In one of the bars where I worked, I got so much slagging about my drinking that I accepted the challenge of staying off the booze for a day. The days turned into weeks. I still managed to avoid drinking, despite the temptation of seeing bottles of spirits everywhere I looked in the bar. This period of sobriety helped my studies no end. Remarkably, I stayed sober for over a year.

I passed the examination, which meant that I was now in a position to apply to university. True to my vow, however drunken, I did apply to various colleges and, eventually, managed to secure a place at University College Cork (UCC), to study law. The day I received my offer was one of the most thrilling of my life. I couldn't wait to tell Deirdre, who was full of pride about my achievement. I look upon that night we spent talking as what Oprah Winfrey calls a 'lightbulb moment' in my life, and I will always be thankful to Deirdre for her patience and common sense.

The only problem was how to come up with the fees. I went to banks for loans but nothing was forthcoming. Part-time work, especially in the precarious world of entertainment, made me a poor risk. I remembered the times as a child when I'd answered the door for my mother and made excuses as to why she couldn't make her repayments. Nothing seemed to change, at least when it came to escaping a poverty-stricken environment. Despite the strides I'd made, it all came down to money and, on this occasion, it was preventing me from accepting my place at university.

One night, a friend in the pub asked me to help him with a disco. I was an experienced DJ and had often earned a few quid on the turntables, but I knew that whatever money came my way wasn't going to get me to UCC. However, I agreed to help him out. My year of being sober came to an end that night. I hit the bottle and awoke the following morning with the mother and father of hangovers. I felt that I was back in the army again, only this time we were marching inside my head. To top it all, I heard someone pounding on the front door and it was only eight o'clock in the morning. I crossed to the window and looked out. My friend from the previous night was standing outside. In no mood to be sociable, I pushed open the window and leaned out. My face said it all.

'I need to see you,' he shouted. I knew what that was about. It was one of the drawbacks of DJing – you had to come back the following day and remove speakers, lights and amps.

'Fuck off,' I shouted back. 'If it's about lifting the gear, I'll do it later.'

'It's not about the gear,' he replied. 'I need to see you now.'

Reluctantly, I came down the stairs and opened the door. He was grinning from ear to ear. 'You won a car in the GAA draw last night, you lucky bastard,' he shouted.

I'd been in a draw for a few years, but had never won a thing, and assumed they were having a laugh. 'I'm going back to bed.'

'No, seriously. You won.' He pulled me outside, where his sister was waiting. She confirmed the fact that I had indeed won a car. I reeled from surprise as I tried to take in the news. If the army marching inside my head wasn't in danger of knocking me over, I'd have turned somersaults along the road there and then.

A few days later, I was given a choice. Take the car, or the cash equivalent of £4,500. I didn't have to think for a second. Already, mentally, my bags were packed. I was heading off to university.

My luck had finally turned. It seemed at last as if some divine intervention was at work – my father or Declan perhaps. It was a nice thought and one I contemplated as I cashed my cheque and began life as a mature student. The Faculty of Law is one of the original faculties of UCC, which was founded in 1845. The university is believed to have a connection to Cork's patron saint, St Finbar, whose monastery and school of learning were in the area, and I enjoyed the feeling that I was immersed in an area renowned for scholarship. I had taken a giant step further away from my past life and, at times, walking through the wooded university grounds or studying in the hushed library, it seemed impossible to associate the furtive grime of one with the polished assurance of the other.

Studying was challenging but fascinating. I was conscious that, at twenty-six years of age, I was the oldest student in my year and wanted desperately to make up for lost time. I discovered I had a love of learning that had never been properly tapped before, and I particularly enjoyed debating. I got involved in student politics and chaired the Mature Student Association.

My love life was colourful and chaotic. By now, I realised that nothing in my life was going to be straightforward, particularly when it came to women. Shea's companion of the night of the brandished bottle had been correct when he told me I was straight. My encounter with Sarah, once we had gotten over the initial problems, had further assured me of my sexual identity. But I found it difficult to establish a lasting, loving relationship with any woman. Over the years, I would gravitate towards women with whom I had no prospect of any kind of stability or future. Sometimes they were married or had drink problems. I would inevitably drive away any woman I met who offered me security, kindness and love. My external life was changing in a positive way, but my internal self was as destructive as ever. I seemed incapable of holding on to a healthy, loving relationship and betrayed several women who would have been excellent life partners.

There were two forces at play: my past and my drinking habit, yet both were so intertwined that they formed a mutual crutch. I could blame everything that went wrong in my life on my past and drown my sorrows yet again in alcohol.

So, the path ahead would be winding, and I continued to drink heavily throughout my college years.

One evening, having spent a day in bed recovering from a hangover, I cycled from my flat in Ballincollig into the college library. On my return a few hours later, heading along a dark lonely stretch of road, I suddenly found myself flying over the handlebars of my bike. I hadn't noticed a pothole in the road, and my front wheel had gone down into it, then twisted badly. I was catapulted onto the tarmac and landed on it with my bare head.

My next memory was of waking up in Cork University Hospital and seeing my mother and some of my sisters at my bedside. I had suffered an extradural haematoma, or brain haemorrhage, leading to a stroke. I had to have emergency surgery to drill a hole in my skull. This, I later discovered, was a craniotomy and was done to relieve the pressure and prevent certain death. I also discovered that I had partial paralysis on the right side of my body. I couldn't feel or move my right leg, arm or side of my face.

My face was black and blue, and I had forty staples in the top and side of my head. I looked like a patchwork quilt and had no desire to gaze overly long at my reflection. I remained in hospital for several weeks, slowly relearning the basics: how to eat, sit up and move. When I walked, I had to drag my right leg behind me. The pins had to stay in my head for a long time after the operation, and I was told I had to recuperate. With few options, I went to stay with one of my sisters, with whom I had never got on. It was a difficult time, and my recovery was slow and painful.

My brush with death gave me no option but to stop and think. But I was a young man in a hurry, trying to make up for lost years. I was conscious that I was the oldest student on my course and was eager about getting back to study. I knew, only too well, how easy it was to fall behind academically and how difficult it was to catch up. As it panned out, the time I had lost put me so far behind in my coursework that I was forced to retake my second year.

This was another blow. I would have to find the money for an extra year and my qualifying would also be delayed. What was more, I would not be with the same student group. Despite everything, however, I was determined to go on. Once again, Deirdre's help and advice were to prove invaluable. I managed to scrape the money together to repeat second year by staying with her in London and working as a porter in an East End hospital, a job her husband secured for me.

Though physically scarred from my injuries, I was now feeling much stronger. I took up my drinking and womanising where I'd left it off, with renewed gusto. I guess I felt I had some catching up to do. I did, however, manage to complete my degree successfully on the new schedule, two years later.

To qualify as a solicitor, you have to be 'indentured' to a practising, qualified solicitor and then pass more exams before you can practise yourself. This process of finding ourselves an apprenticeship kicked off at the beginning of third year. I didn't really understand what was involved until I began the search for a practice in which to serve it. I approached solicitor after solicitor, to no avail. It appeared I came from the wrong social background.

I resorted to being 'resourceful' and began to approach solicitors posing as someone seeking legal advice. Once my foot was in the door, and I was sitting opposite them, I would lay out my case. Eventually, my unconventional ploy worked, and I was successful in being taken on by an established lawyer. He drove a hard bargain and, as was common practice for apprentices, I would not be paid much. But it enabled me to finish off my training and ultimately become a fully fledged lawyer. My dream had come true.

I qualified from UCC in 1994 and became a fully fledged solicitor in 1997, a total of almost seven years of hard work. Against all the odds, I had proved to myself that I could amount to something and felt very proud as I accepted my degree.

My own personal life, however, was still staggering from crisis to crisis. Despite my near-death experience, and my professional achievements, my drinking continued to escalate.

One drunken night, having lost my keys, I climbed back into my digs through a window, sending the contents of the windowsill crashing to the floor in my wake. A good friend, seeing the mess I was in, gave me black coffee and talked to me until dawn broke about what I was doing to myself. It turned out he himself had gone to AA many years before. I'd known him for some time, but this was news to me. It proved once again that it's impossible to know what story lies behind a smiling face. I listened to him and tried to sober up. He was someone I respected, and I admired what he had achieved through sobriety. But what did it have to do with me? I simply couldn't face the truth. Things would have to get a lot worse before they could get any better.

I was finishing my third year at university and beginning my apprenticeship when I met the woman whom, for the purposes of the story, I will call Marjory. It was a tough but exciting time in my life and, as was my wont, I was working hard and playing hard. The attraction to Marjory had been instant and strong, and soon we were living together. I was convinced Marjory was the one.

We came through a lot of ups and downs in my early days of learning the trade and establishing my own business. My relationship with Marjory gave me a reason to focus on my career, and on establishing a proper home. When she announced she was pregnant, I was ecstatic. And when our beautiful daughter was born, it was an absolute miracle to me. I felt unspeakable happiness and a sense of pure wonder simply looking into her cot at her angelic face and watching as she grew and began to take her first steps.

But, sadly, soon enough relations between myself and Marjory began to unravel. By now, I had a heavy case-load and a thriving practice. But I was still drinking heavily, and burning the candle both ends. I had recently been admitted to hospital with pleurisy. I had always suffered from asthma, and smoking had done nothing to ease the problem. Everyone has a weak point that acts up when they are stressed. With me, it was my chest. When I was stressed as a child, I often got bronchitis or pneumonia. Not surprisingly, I was often ill. As I grew older, I managed to control my health but, inevitably, my chest was the barometer of my emotional state.

On this occasion, there were medical complications, and I was soon suffering from both pleurisy and pneumonia. I was desperate to get back to work, as I needed to stay afloat. I hadn't struggled so hard to get to where I was at in order to see everything fall apart through ill health.

On the day I was released from hospital, I drove straight to the office and worked there until eight o'clock at night. Then I drove back to our home in Ennis, a town north of Limerick, in County Clare. When I arrived, I thought it odd that there were no lights on. On entering, I knew instantly that something was very wrong. Marjory had gone, taking my daughter, and the contents of our house, with her.

Empty houses make a certain sound. Doorbells ring too loudly. Footsteps echo. Voices do not answer. I looked around the empty rooms of my large, comfortable home and realised that everyone I loved had disappeared. Many years had passed since the horrors of my past, yet I could not put it behind me, however I yearned to forget. The memories stalked me.

I had scraped the bottom of the barrel many times but, in this moment, as I stood in the empty rooms of the house I had shared with my girlfriend and our beautiful young daughter, I felt that I could sink no further. No matter how often I picked up the pieces and moved forward, I couldn't.

When thoughts of suicide plagued me, that past seemed dangerously close. The temptation to close the book and find peace overwhelmed me. Yet, somehow, I always found the strength to pick up my life and move on with it. But this time? This time, I was not so sure.

Our relationship had not been good for some time. I knew that my drinking, very long working hours and, now, my illness had probably pushed her to the limit. I slipped to my knees on the bare floor of the empty room. There was nothing to cushion the silence. It crushed me, accused me, mocked me.

I called my daughter's name. I knew she would not respond, but I needed to hear it sounding through the emptiness that was left in her wake. It is only when something is lost that its preciousness is fully appreciated, and my daughter was the light of my life.

I'd stopped crying a long time ago. I knew better than most that tears served no purpose whatsoever. But that night, on my knees on the floor, my tears flowed freely. I knew who was to blame for the desolation and loneliness I was feeling.

I could cite a mismatched relationship with Marjory. Despite the difficulties that had grown between us, I had hoped, on some level, that we could hang in there and work things out, now that we were a family. I could cite the stresses of dealing with complex legal cases, constant demands on my time and the pressure to succeed. I could list reasons on the fingers of both hands and still avoid touching the truth. My life was empty for one reason only.

Alcohol. Man's best friend. Life's great obliterator. Without it, the past came too close. Faces swam out of the mire. Danny, Diarmuid, the Dublin duo, the ones whom I'd been with when my taste for spirits had first developed, at the tender age of eleven. How quickly the Dubliners had sussed out the Limerick scene and exploited it to their full advantage. Scotch and red lemonade, I remembered it well. The glow of wellbeing, the easy laughter, the camaraderie as we strutted from the pub on the docks and allowed the night to take us over. I earned my first five pounds at the end of that night. I learned the tricks of the trade without any difficulty. After all, I'd had a long apprenticeship.

Nobody Heard Me Cry

When I could no longer endure the silence of my empty house, I rose to my feet. I locked the front door and did the only thing I could: I went to the pub and drank until the past became bearable again.

19

A New Millennium

Let me carry your Cross for Ireland, Lord!
Let me suffer the pain and shame
I bow my head to their rage and hate,
And I take upon myself the blame.
Let them do with my body whate'er they will,
My spirit I offer to You.
That the faithful few who heard her call
May be spared to Roisin Dubh.

From 'Let Me Carry Your Cross for Ireland, Lord!'
by Thomas Ashe

My father's uncle, the patriot Thomas Ashe, wrote these
words in the full knowledge that he could face death for his
belief in a free republic. He was a man with ideals, courage,
determination. His belief that he would sacrifice his life for

254

his cause was duly borne out and he was ennobled in death, enshrined in memory. He was part of a patriotic wave that created the Republic into which I was born and which I shared with some of the vilest people I would ever encounter.

I had never been able to shake those people from my shoulders, but the dawn of a new millennium seemed like an appropriate time to start. I was consumed by fury, by regret, by the need for revenge, for an explanation, for justice. One face, above all, dominated: Aidan, the bastard who had started the downward spiral and who had broken my resistance.

The moment one walks into a police station is a first step into new territory. But the thought process undertaken before that initial step is torturous. Sometimes, it seems an easier option to let the past die. Why open a can of worms and have to subject oneself to all that will follow once the legal process gets underway?

For me, there were many reasons why I made my decision to make a report against Aidan, my first abuser. Some were clear-cut, such as the desire for justice and retribution, the protection of other potential young victims. Others were less easy to understand, even to myself.

When I was a young boy, I cringed in dread every time I passed this man. I was now a mature adult, in control of my life, or so I liked to believe. Yet, I still cringed when I saw him. His very presence had the power to transform me back again into that terrified child, and I could no longer endure it. By making a formal complaint against my abuser, I hoped to begin to heal myself.

I also needed courage to move forward. At an early age, I had been broken and groomed for a life I despised. For many complex reasons, it had taken me years to find the courage to break away from that circle of vice. Only for the kindness of my friend, Paddy Mullins, who led me into the army, I may never have discovered there were other options in life. Courage is something I had to fight for and, when I entered the garda station on this chilly, grey day, I hoped it would not desert me.

I made a full statement to the gardaí, outlining what had taken place with Aidan beginning when I was an eight-year-old boy and lasting for almost three years. The details of that first abuse were still vivid, easy to recall, yet difficult to give voice to. An understanding sergeant took my statement. The process took three hours. I'd known it was going to be tough but had not reckoned that the pain of reliving the assaults would become almost unbearable.

I was astonished at how emotional I became as I revealed the details of the abuse in all its tawdry detail, and I was reduced to helpless tears on several occasions. The veneer of adulthood is a thin protection when traumas and memories are unresolved. My mother also made a statement confirming that I had told her about the abuse many years before.

The process I had set in motion would prove to be a slow

and torturous one. No information would be forthcoming until a decision was made by the Director of Public Prosecutions (DPP), as to whether or not a case could proceed. All I could do was wait in the hope that a full investigation was underway and the truth would finally be revealed.

Around a year later, I was still anxiously awaiting word as to whether or not the DPP would proceed to prosecute Aidan. On this occasion, I was having a drink in a local pub. There were two off-duty guards I recognised sitting nearby. Slagging is part and parcel of pub culture. Sometimes it can be a well-intended joke, but then one man's joke is another man's insult. On this occasion, the joke was on me, and the two men were enjoying my discomfort. According to them, the case would never see the light of day.

I laughed off their opinions. What did they know? But they repeated the fact that, because I was representing leading criminals, the gardaí would drop the investigation. Although I did not take them at their word, their comments raised alarm bells in my head, and I was unable to shake off my uneasiness.

Five months later, a detective sergeant from the station in question rang to formally inform me that the DPP had decided not to proceed with my case. As is usual in such decisions, no reason was forthcoming. At first, I was struck dumb: I refused to believe what I was hearing. Finally, I managed to speak. 'Two gardaí told me this would happen.

They said it's because I am representing the wrong families, isn't it? It's true what they said.'

'That's rubbish,' the Sergeant replied. 'The decision was taken by the DPP, not by us.'

The Sergeant was sympathetic to my position. He listened patiently while I raged over the phone, then advised me to let it go. In my anger, I spoke of how I would now have to see to it that justice was done, in my own way. He talked me down: what was the sense in throwing away my career and everything I'd accomplished over the years by doing something reckless?

But I had to fight hard against the urge not to take a hammer and smash it against my abuser's head. That was simply how I felt. Since I was eight years old, I'd lived with the pain of those encounters, and now, thirty years later, Aidan would not even have to stand in the dock and face his victim. I was sick walking the same streets as him, knowing he was sneering at me every time he passed me by, still holding on to a small vestige of corrupted power, all these decades later.

These feelings were to crystallise one evening, shortly after I'd received the news. I was stopped at traffic lights, on my way home from work. Another car pulled up beside mine. I glanced over and instantly recognised the driver. It was Aidan. He grinned openly over at me and gave me the finger. He might as well have leaned out the window and shouted

'Fuck off!' In no uncertain terms, he was telling me what he thought of my efforts to bring him to trial.

Nothing could have held me back. Incandescent with rage, I leapt from my own car to the driver's side of his and began beating with all my might against the window, trying to smash my way in to him. Had I succeeded, I truly believe I would have torn his heart out.

Aidan had showed me, in the most blatant way possible, his contempt for my attempts to bring him to justice. I knew the routine that took place when such an allegation was made against an individual. He would have been subjected to a rigorous cross-examination at the garda station. Mine had taken over three hours. How long had his taken? I had no way of knowing, but what was perfectly clear to me was that both statements had been scrutinised by the office of the DPP – and a decision had been made. My abuser was off the hook.

And now, here he was, openly mocking me, pumped up and proud in his triumph. I continued to beat furiously at the windows. Aidan didn't look quite so self-satisfied now, as he hurriedly obeyed the light's signal change and sped off.

That evening, I returned to my empty home, still seething, not knowing what I was capable of. I did the only thing I knew: I drank. It's no coincidence that so many suicides take place after a person has been drinking heavily. And I should know. I had attempted suicide once when I was a young lad, and I walked constantly in its shadow since then.

That night, I diced with death for the second time in my

life. As before, I used alcohol and tablets and, again, it was a cry for help. Before I went too far, my survival instinct kicked in, and I phoned a friend, whom I knew to be a member of AA. We talked for several hours on the phone. I stayed conscious and kept moving until I was over the worst of the effects. Somehow, I had to find the means to accept that I, like many others who try to take cases against their abusers, had failed.

As that dark night gave rise to a new day, I prayed. In truth, by this stage of my life I had little belief in God or the power of prayer. How could a merciful God allow such injustice to thrive and prosper? This logical argument was no match against my urge to pray, and the more I prayed, the more sincere my prayers became. A phrase of my mothers – 'This too shall pass' – came unbidden into my head. I repeated it like a mantra.

My friends and members of my family had witnessed my gradual deterioration: the regular benders, the blackouts, the succession of destructive affairs. On one occasion, one of my sisters, who had trained as a counsellor as part of her nursing qualification, arranged to meet me for dinner. Any illusion I had that we were going to have a meal together was quickly dispelled when she announced that she intended taking me to an AA meeting.

This decision, however well intentioned, was like a red rag to a bull. I lost my head with her. How dare she make assumptions about me, shove her opinions down my throat? She hadn't lived my life. How could she appreciate what I had gone through, why I needed drink, to keep a lid on things. When I had needed her, where had she been? I asked. I had all the excuses lined up, along with a good dollop of self-pity. We argued bitterly, and the more she tried to persuade me to consider AA, the more defensive I became.

Eventually, she gave up. We didn't speak for days, but she met with me again and apologised. She accepted that she had made a mistake in trying to coerce me to attend the AA meeting and should have respected my right to make my own decision. She added, 'John, don't make a mistake of shutting down your mind to this completely. I think it would be useful for you to go to AA, and if you ever wanted to go and wanted my assistance, I'd help any way I could.'

This was a gesture that reached out to me, and I appreciated this. I seriously began to think about her advice. Of course, I knew about AA. Other people had talked to me about how it functioned, which, as far as I was concerned, was fine for them. But it was not for me. I was different.

It would take some courage to actually get there but, eventually, I found myself going through the doors of my first meeting. The minute I took that first step, I felt like I was returning home.

It was difficult at first. I sat and listened to others for a long time before I was able to speak. The idea of putting down my drink and never picking it up again seemed inconceivable. It was both terrifying and a relief – two contrasting emotions that I would have to work out for myself. My first few months in AA were spent drinking less, switching spirits for beer and evading the problem in a number of ways. As Abraham Lincoln once said, 'You can fool some of the people all of the time, and all of the people some of the time, but you cannot fool all of the people all of the time.' To that I would add: a drinking alcoholic fools himself most of all – and he does it all the time.

When it was obvious I was only fooling myself about seriously giving up drink totally, my sponsor, Tony, took me aside and laid it on the line. I was wasting my time unless I took AA seriously. 'If you can't stop drinking for one day, concentrate on not drinking for one hour, or for ten minutes, or even just for two minutes, if that is what it takes to get you through,' he said. Those words stuck with me, and I now apply them to each day of my life.

The desire to keep the channel open with Marjory, and therefore my daughter, was a major spur in helping me to kick the habit. I had always made sure my daughter never saw me drunk, and I wanted to keep it that way. Also, I did not want my daughter to be another child whose father had simply dropped off the map. I knew what it was like to grow up without a father. I remembered how I used to look at other, happier families and envy their togetherness. I was determined that my daughter would not grow up and face the same loss. I would provide for her, in every way, and maintain a strong presence in her life. In order to do that, in the right way, I had to kick the drink.

I was also anxious to avoid getting into debt and to break the pattern of difficult relationships. The urge to build a successful business was also uppermost in my mind. It would have been so easy for me to, literally, piss it all away.

Shortly after I joined AA, I met someone who was to radically change the course of my life for the better. Julieann, who is now my wife, worked as a receptionist for the Limerick *Evening Echo* and our relationship grew in a natural and unhurried way. We became good friends before we became lovers, but I knew from early on that we were soulmates. She has been with me in my struggle to get sober, and her encouragement has been vital. The rub of my back, the stroking of my hair, the making of true love.

Throughout my journey to sobriety, Julieann remained a wonderful support and was by my side on the night I celebrated my fortieth birthday. She had planned a surprise party for me. It would be held in a city centre pub and all my friends were sworn to secrecy. Has anyone who ever had a surprise party really been surprised? It's a difficult secret to keep and, by the time the day arrived, I was both excited and apprehensive. Would I be able to stay off the drink for the night? I would enter that pub with the firmest of intentions but once the atmosphere built up and the craic got going, I could easily give in and convince myself that one celebratory drink would do no harm.

I had a hectic day at work. We were in the middle of a high-profile case with one of my clients, and I had been over and back to the garda station three times that afternoon. Then I rushed home for a shave and a shower, knowing I would be back to the court again for a second sitting before I got a chance to attend my surprise party.

Julieann collected me outside the courthouse and, by the time we arrived at the pub, the party was already in full swing. The atmosphere was familiar, and the longing to be in the middle of it, knocking back the drinks, cracking jokes, ordering another round, hit me immediately. I called upon God to help me through the hours to come. My Higher Power did come to my aid, but I had to call on him many times before the night was over.

This proved to be one of my biggest challenges. So many people wanted to buy me a drink. I kept refusing. Some close friends persisted. They were so insistent that I took them aside and explained that I was now a recovering alcoholic. Immediately, the offers of drink dried up. People became very supportive when they understood what I was trying to overcome. Indeed, it was around that time that I began to distinguish between my true friends and my so-called drinking buddies.

One particular incident illustrates how far I was able to finally move away from the legacy of my childhood chaos. A couple of years after I joined AA, I was accosted outside

Shannon Court by a former client, who was also an alcoholic. I was no longer doing this particular court on a regular basis, and therefore had stopped representing him. Seeing me there now, he got angry and began to threaten me. Eventually, I had to make a complaint to gardaí, and he was taken into custody. A short time later, he was brought before the judge. He had some difficulty with his solicitor, who was unable to represent him.

Although I was there to give evidence against this man, I took pity on him. I was familiar with the bleak depths of alcoholism and the loneliness that always accompanied it, even in the most crowded pub. There and then I decided that, should he want me to do so, I would represent him in court. Despite the inescapable irony of my having called the guards on him to begin with, I whispered to the man, who was drunk at the time, that I was a recovering alcoholic and that he too could receive help from AA. Unfortunately, he was too confused to register the fact that I was trying to help him.

In court, the arresting garda stood up and gave his evidence against the man. I was then asked to give evidence. I explained to the judge that I had indeed been threatened that morning by the man in question. Since then, I reassured the judge, we had shaken hands, and I had spoken to him about his alcoholism.

'I am particularly well suited to do so,' I told the judge, who peered at me incredulously over his glasses. He asked me why this was so.

Should I say anything in public about my own case? I swallowed hard and began nervously to speak. 'I could put him in touch with the fellowship of Alcoholics Anonymous and, in fact, with my own sponsor.'

There was a stunned silence in the court. 'I am a member of AA myself,' I announced, wanting there to be no ambiguity. The judge shuffled his papers and announced he was adjourning the case.

Whether making this admission as I had was right or wrong, I don't know, but I actually felt relieved. By telling the judge I was a fellow alcoholic, I was accepting, publicly, who I was. And I was in a position to help someone in a similar position. It was unorthodox, maybe even unwise, but by then I thought, What the hell, this is my life, and I have to lead it this way.

When the case resumed, the judge sentenced the man to seven days in jail and referred him to an addiction centre for treatment. At this point, I asked the judge if I might represent the man. The judge asked him if he would like me to represent him, and the man agreed immediately. I pleaded passionately with the judge to give him a second chance. As a consequence, his time in prison was reduced to four days. After further pleadings, the sentence was suspended entirely, on the condition that he agreed to go to AA. He did.

I felt pleased with a job well done.

Epilogue

If you learn as a child that you don't deserve love, it's very hard to accept love in later life. For years, my adult life was characterised by this failure of love: my failure to love myself, and my failure to thrive in a healthy loving relationship. With Julieann, it was different. With Julieann, I blossomed. She became my rock: sexy, funny, great company. Often she would drive out to an AA meeting with me. Some of the meetings were in Foynes, a beautiful port on the Shannon Estuary twenty miles from Limerick. She would wait for me there, and we would take a stroll through the harbour afterwards. On other occasions, I would later discover, she would follow me to a meeting, just to make sure I was sticking with the programme. I will always be so grateful to have had someone behind me who was so concerned for my wellbeing.

Julieann and I got married on 29 March, 2007, and had our reception at Bunratty Manor, in the stunning surroundings of County Clare. It was a wonderful occasion, and a party of eighty of our closest loved ones gathered to share it with us. My mother was there, and my sister Deirdre along with her husband, and various relatives and friends who had been of great support to me over the years.

At times, I wonder what I have done to deserve Julieann. I'm probably not what you'd call natural husband material. I'm me, after all. But there is something about my wife that is different. I am sober now and, for the first time, a married man. We now have a young daughter and, for the first time in my life, a proper home life.

My own struggle with alcohol was not an easy one. I had many slips and falls off the proverbial wagon but, eventually, I was able to stop drinking completely. I have been sober now for six years. Sobriety is a step-by-step process and, even now, I give thanks daily that I am able to cope, for that day only.

As I write this book, the process of getting my life back on track, and dealing with the ghosts of my past, is still unfolding. It is a slow and often painful journey. Only when I stopped abusing my body and brain could I begin to work out who I really was. Viewing the world without the haze of alcohol has meant that, rather than running from my past, I now have a chance to get to grips with it in a real and honest way. I guess everything has its time, and things come when you are ready for them.

The damaged child inside me who had, for all these years, kicked and reeled in a bid to make the world sit up and pay attention to his plight has finally found a voice. I can experience true emotion now in a way that was not possible before.

These days, my relationship with my mother is very different to what it was in times past, though we still have our ups and downs. But we have an understanding. I recognise now, in a way that I could not as a child, the challenges that she faced, as a young widow with seven children to look after, then, tragically, six.

As the phrase goes, the past is a different country. And, in writing this book, I take a significant step in laying mine to rest. Times are easier now, and I have a brighter future to look forward to. But there is no escaping the bitter legacy of those years. I give thanks daily that I pulled through and that when I diced with my life, death was looking the other way. I got a second chance to make something of my life – for myself and for my cherished loved ones.

I take the most wonderful pride in my two beautiful daughers – my older one from my earlier relationship with Marjory and my daughter with Julieann. They are the best of friends, happy, safe, confident, provided for in a warm, loving environment. It is a thousand miles away from where I started, in the rough, tough roads of Janesboro.

As for work and career, Paddy Mullins certainly set me on the right path by getting me into the army. My move into the law I see, on one level, as stemming from a sense of injustice and burning anger at the wrongs that I had myself experienced. I had a deep well from my own childhood to tap into, but I was also driven by a desire to fight a corner for the people society leaves behind: the poor, the uneducated, the underprivileged, the trafficked children, the abused women – all the kids exploited for another's gain and satisfaction. As I said at the outset of this journey, not everyone was as lucky as me. Not everyone survived.

During the 1980s, revelations about sexual abuse and the clergy began to come out. Father Denis Daly, the first priest I had been paid to 'service' in the dockland's toilet, all those years ago, had many victims. Peter McCloskey was one of them. Peter was an intelligent, sensitive young man who should have had a bright future ahead of him.

In 2002, Peter approached me. As described in the foreword of this book, he was attempting to find out whether the diocese of Limerick had reason to suspect that Father Daly might have been a danger to children. His efforts were being met with closed doors. Knowing that I was a fellow victim, he wanted me to come forward with my story. There was strength in numbers, and the more people who spoke out, the harder it would be for the Catholic Church to keep shutting its doors on the truth.

I was still running from my past, and still reeling from my failure to secure a prosecution for Aidan. If the Church ever did admit to knowledge of Father Daly's history of abuse, and it ever got as far as a legal action, the notion that the legal system offered protection or justice in this area seemed to me, at best, farcical. If life had taught me anything, it was that there were no consequences for abusers. I told Peter that I was sorry, but I wasn't in a position to do as he asked.

When, soon after his failed battle to secure the truth, Peter tragically took his own life, I felt steeped in guilt. I had let down a friend and fellow sufferer of abuse in his time of greatest need. And the circumstances seemed to epitomise perfectly that feeling of helplessness, of powerlessness, that so dogged my life and the lives of so many victims of abuse: of being damned if you do, and damned if you don't.

I now work as a criminal defence lawyer in Limerick District Court. I represent people who have been unfairly treated or who have gotten into trouble because of their own family background, or lack of education, or hopeless addiction – whatever it is that has led them into murky criminal waters. I am able to identify with these people, as I know where they come from. I may represent guys high on drugs, or women who have knifed someone whom they believe has done them wrong – the kind of people who are considered the dregs of society, not worth a thought. But I know that when I stand up in court and defend them, I am defending people who have acted, possibly, out of sheer desperation, out of fear and poverty, people whose lives are often a complete mess and who are completely alienated from mainstream society. I try and do my best for them and, in my own small way, I am trying to make things better for those who feel there is absolutely no way out of their own particular ghetto.

I now try to be a Paddy Mullins to those who have never had one themselves, nor even a decent father, mother or any other reliable adult to give them discipline and direction.

Which brings me back to Seamus Connery, and where this whole story began.

Seamus was sitting sweating into his flamboyant suit in the Henry Street interview room at that midnight hour. I left him contemplating what he might plead, given that I knew full well what he was capable of doing. It had happened several times after that initial meeting, too, as Seamus continued to pick up the 'chemist's son' whenever he fancied some fresh 'chicken' for his bedtime treat.

As I left Seamus in the interview room, I thanked God that I was now sober enough, strong enough and big enough to sit with this man and work with him. Here, thirty years later, Seamus Connery was still plying boys with wine for illegal sexual favours. That's a hell of a lot of 'chicken' to have been abused over three decades.

Right away, I knew there was a conflict of interest in my acting for him if he maintained the lie. But I explained that if he wanted to tell the truth I would help him professionally as much as I could. Seamus Connery duly confessed. This was not due to coercion on my part. He was brought to court and charged with committing a sexual assault on a minor. As he pleaded 'Guilty, Judge', my heart lifted. I retained my professional demeanour but took pleasure in watching my client having to admit to the 'error' of his ways.

He was convicted and ordered to go on a course for sex offenders at Barnardo's, to prevent him from reoffending. There are no certainties, and everyone knows that paedophiles don't change overnight, but Seamus Connery would now be a registered sex offender, monitored for the rest of his natural life. Hopefully, he would never terrorise any other young boys sexually again. Hopefully.

For me, the damage has been done, and there is no going back. Not a day goes by when I do not feel the effects of those years of abuse. Ultimately, I know there is no way of breaking free completely from the chains of my past. But I am on a slow, steady journey back to myself and, every day, I get a little bit closer. Life feels good. And if I can do anything in my power as a adult to stop the next child becoming a victim at the hands of the likes of Seamus Connery, then the struggle will have been worthwhile.

Acknowledgements

To my beautiful wife Julieann, who had been most patient with me throughout the time that the book was being written, re-written and re-written.

To my two children, whom I love dearly, the eldest of whom knows a lot about my life and who has supported me in my endeavours to get the book published, and to my youngest daughter who could be always heard in the background of Dictaphone tape when the work was being put together.

To my mother, who had the most difficult of circumstances cast upon her forty-five years ago, but who in recent years has worked with me in rebuilding bridges together.

To Anthony Galvin, writer and journalist, without whose advice, assistance and re-writing this book would never have come to life.

To Corinne Sweet, who helped me tell my story.

To Michelle Cosgrave, who adopted the book as a labour of love and more particularly a special thanks for all the sleepless nights she spent in the office typing the original manuscript. I will never forget her trust, friendship and loyalty. I also thank Caroline Higgins of my office who helped Michelle when she was at her wits end trying to get the manuscript together.

I also thank all of the office staff who performed their professional duties whilst assisting me in the book: Michelle Cosgrave, Caroline Higgins, Marguerite Freney, Des Newman, Julieann Stanley (Devane), Michael Quain, Katie Freney and Siobhan Higgins. I would also like to thank Martin Cosgrave of You're a Star fame, who helped us voluntarily in our reception when we were up the walls working on the book and his cousin was getting no sleep by night.

A special sincere thanks extends to John O'Dwyer, without whose help, life and business would have been a lot more difficult; and also to his wife Breda and their daughter.

A sincere mention must be given to Catherine Cahill of the Late Late Show, who I first spoke to about this book and who, when given a copy of the manuscript, pointed me in the direction that would ultimately see the book being published.

Thanks to my cousins Catherine and Biddy and their families for their unstinting support over many years.

A special thanks is due to my editor at Hachette Books Ireland, Ciara Considine, who worked long and tedious hours in the final preparation of the book, and to all the staff there, especially Breda, Jim and Margaret.

A special thanks is given to Helen Coyle of Hodder & Stoughton in London who had faith in the work the moment she read it and flew over to Ireland to meet me.

A special thanks to the late Dolores Winters of Shannon, County Clare, who was a close and valued friend and who encouraged me to try and bring this to light for the purpose of helping others.

A special thanks has to be given to Doctor Frieda Keane Carmody and her husband Paschal Carmody for their medical intervention at a time when I had contracted MRSA and they discovered a tumour growing in my throat, although this had been missed by others.

To John and Joan Morgan and their children Gearoid and Ciara, a grateful and sincere thanks for being best friends and extremely supportive in good, bad and lean times.

A word of gratitude extends to the fellowship of AA who shun publicity but without whom I would probably not be alive.

To Michael Maloney B.L. and his wife Kathleen who continued to encourage me to bring this book to fruition.

To Brian McInerney B.L. and his wife Sharon for their continuing support and a special word of thanks to Brian who has always tried to steer me clear of troubled waters both in the writing of this book and in my career as a solicitor.

To all the District and Circuit Court staff in Limerick City and County who encouraged me every step of the way with the book and life within the court system. To the District Court Clerks who regularly brought me back into life and ensured that I did not lose my temperament: Eileen, Valerie, Marie, Ken, Josephine and the two Peters and the rest of the staff.

To all the solicitors who assisted me over the years in the District Court and more particularly Sarah Ryan Solicitor.

The late Mr. Justice Sean O'Leary who protected, helped and advised me in relation to my work as a solicitor both when he was a Circuit Court Judge and a Judge of the High Court.

A grateful acknowledgement also extends to Judge Michael Reilly, who spoke to me in his chambers one day for a couple of hours and who taught me more in that time than I had learnt over many years as a practitioner in Limerick District Court.

The Management and Staff and all their families of the Bunratty Manor, who have had to listen to my dreams, aspirations and ambition about bringing this book to life over the last few years.

A special thanks and gratitude extends to Tony (whose name I have permission to use) who brought me to my first AA meeting and who brought me down to ground and kept me sane when I needed to lose my ego.

My sponsor in AA who is like an Angel on my shoulder, ever prodding me when I step out of line.

To Julieann's auntie Joan O'Brien (and her family) who has been like a mother to Julieann since her own mother tragically died, and who accepted me into their family, warts and all.

To Mrs. Mary Fortune and her daughter Olivia and their extended family, who were my second family for many years.

To Harry Gleeson, the first bank manager to have faith in me, and his wife Bernadette. Also thanks to my accountant Tim Dennehy, who worked closely with Harry Gleeson and my office to allow us time to finish this project.

To Mary Rogan Manager of the Bank of Ireland, Limerick, for all her support.

To Lorraine and Hazel, our babysitters who looked after my youngest daughter and in their endeavours kept Julieann sane by allowing her to get some time out with her husband, away from the book.

To all of my clients, some of whom have become close friends through all aspects of my work. Aware of my life history, they have stuck by me through all adversity. I cannot for reasons both of a solicitor/client nature and the constrains of space name all of you individually, but you know who you are.

To Mary O'Meara, close friend and confidant, and her family, for all their encouragement with regards to the book.

To my father's sister Maura Cuddihy for all the encouragement she gave me and faith she had in me no matter how bad things were.

And lastly, finally, sincere thanks to my sister Joan, who has always treated me like both a son and a brother, and without whose assistance in life I would not be where I am today. She also assisted me in the writing of this book and clarified details surrounding the time after my birth, which I could never have known otherwise. Also, sincere thanks extend to her husband Graham for all the advice he gave me and for being there like the older brother I never knew.